DEDICATION

Dedicated to the countless leaders whom I have had the chance to learn from along my own professional journey—those I have had the opportunity to lead and be led by, and those whose leadership I've watched from a distance.

And to those leaders out there who share in my quest to create workplaces that bring out people's best.

PRAISE FOR *THE BLUE FLAME*

"In today's knowledge economy, people are everything in business — and lighting them up is the heart of a leader's role. Your employees are the foundation that your company's success is built on, and if they aren't operating at full power, neither will your business. Learn how to unlock your company's potential with *The Blue Flame!*"

—Marshall Goldsmith, *New York Times* #1 Bestselling Author and Only Two-Time #1 Leadership Thinker in the World

"The most important ingredient of a company is its people, and *The Blue Flame* homes in on how to align every individual's talents, passions, and deep sense of purpose to create a world where employees don't just love their jobs, they also excel at them. Imagine if every company could operate this way!"

—Julie Zhuo, Author of *Wall Street Journal* Bestseller *The Making of a Manager*

"Dan Cremons has done it. His book, *The Blue Flame*, offers practical tools on how to unleash the potential in others. Read Dan's book and you will learn how to ignite the natural talents, passion, and purpose within every person and team... and how doing so can translate into real results for your business."

—Michael K. Simpson, Amazon Bestselling Author, *Powerful Leadership Through Coaching and Unlocking Potential*

"Having been in the leadership development space for over 26 years, it is super exciting and thrilling to come across a new book that totally nails it...in its context, its content and its applicability...and with the bonus of great storytelling. This brilliant new work by Dan Cremons is one of those books. I cannot recommend this book enough for every member of your organization."

—Rick Tamlyn, Author of *Play Your Bigger Game*, Expert in Human Development, and F100 Advisor

© 2020 by Dan Cremons

Names and details of some individuals have been changed to preserve their privacy. The opinions in this book are the author's and do not represent any other organization. This book is intended for information only.

Library of Congress Cataloging Information available upon request.

First Softcover Edition

10 9 8 7 6 5 4 3 2 1

Printed in the United States
Produced and Edited by Raab & Co. | www.Raabandco.com

ISBN: 979-8-6728213-6-8

DAN CREMONS

THE BLUE FLAME

THE REMARKABLY SIMPLE IDEA THAT CAN
TRANSFORM YOUR LEADERSHIP
AND **IGNITE YOUR TEAM**

Contents

INTRODUCTION TO THE BLUE FLAME

What Is the Blue Flame?	**10**
A New Kind of Fuel	**22**
"This Could Change Everything"	**40**

TALENTS: DO WHAT YOU DO BEST

What Can You Do Best?	**58**
Discovering Our Talents	**78**
But What About Our Weaknesses?	**90**

PASSIONS: DO WHAT MOST INVIGORATES YOU

What Makes You Come Alive?	**116**
Discover What Invigorates You	**122**

PURPOSE: DO WHAT YOU CARE DEEPLY ABOUT

What Do You Care Deeply About?	**146**

INTO ACTION

Put a Ding in the Universe	**166**
Blue Flame Conversations	**180**

ACKNOWLEDGMENTS   **208**

PART 01

Introduction to the Blue Flame

CHAPTER 1

What Is the Blue Flame?

> **HERE'S THE BIG IDEA IN 102 WORDS:**
>
> Amazing things happen when you play at the intersection point of three powerful forces:
>
> - Your Talents: what you can do best.
> - Your Passions: activities that invigorate you.
> - Your Purpose: what you care deeply about.
>
> When these forces collide, a powerful chemical reaction called the Blue Flame can be ignited. The Blue Flame has the power to ignite careers, to turbocharge companies, and—dare I be so bold—to change the world. And there hasn't been a more important time than now for leaders and their teams to lean into the performance-enhancing, life-altering, growth-accelerating, world-changing power of the Blue Flame.

This book was written primarily for people in leadership roles. The research-backed and battle-tested ideas that we will explore in this book can help you to get the best out of your people, and in doing so, make their life and your company richer. If you're like me, getting the best out of your people that they have to give probably matters to you quite a bit, as leaders who are up to big, important things need a team of people who have come alive.

The ideas that follow are rooted in four fundamental beliefs that leaders hoping to harness the power of the Blue Flame in their business should embrace. Before passing go, it is important that we level-set here.

Belief #1: Every person is exceedingly talented in their own way.
Sometimes, people themselves don't know their talents or don't use them fully. As we will discuss in Chapter 4 there can be some real psychological and

cognitive impediments to understanding our own talents. But great Blue Flame leaders, those who get the best that their people have to give, believe that there's extraordinary talent to be found, unearthed, and unleashed in every person.

Belief #2: The role and responsibility of a leader is to help unleash this talent.
Blue Flame leaders feel a strong sense of responsibility to help each of their people discover their own Blue Flame, and apply it in a way that can have big impact. They view themselves as the *catalysts* who spark the reaction between an employee's talents, passions, and purpose, and the goals of the organization. Leaders who are up to big things need to get the best out of those around them. As you will see in Chapter 11, Blue Flame conversations can be invaluable in helping leaders to do this.

Belief #3: Companies should exist to enhance the lives of those they serve, starting with their *employees*.
Companies, and the leaders who lead them, should embrace a strong sense of responsibility and commitment to making the workplace a force for good in the lives of their employees. Research has shown that employees who work in enriching workplaces reward their employers with higher levels of productivity, greater loyalty, and ultimately, better business performance. Blue Flame leaders understand that building a culture that puts their people's talents to good use, crafts their role around work they find invigorating, and helps them find meaning in the work is *integral* to maximizing profits, rather than in opposition to it.

Belief #4: The world would be a better place if every person lived and worked in alignment with their Blue Flame.
If everyone was working and living in alignment with their Blue Flame, within their business and beyond, imagine the problems we could solve, the codes we could crack, and the tough challenges we could overcome.

I can distinctly recollect the first time I saw the video of comedian and actor Jim Carrey's original 1980 *Saturday Night Live* audition. I was in stitches, totally bowled over by the performance. At the time of its filming, Carrey was just 17 or 18 years old, and was scraping by as the opening act at a comedy club in Toronto called Yuk Yuk's.

As the cameras started rolling at NBC Studios, Carrey seemed confident and relaxed, despite an environment that must have been far from relaxing, given he was performing for a small and hyper-critical audience of "seen it all before" *SNL* staffers.

Carrey launches into his bid, his opening gambit an impersonation of "post-nuclear" Elvis. You need to see the clip to fully understand the "post-nuclear" aspect, but picture a normal-sized Elvis with hands sticking directly out of his torso.

His perfect Elvis sneer reaches halfway up one side of his face. His hips sway and his legs have taken on that rubbery quality that was so characteristic of Elvis's style. Carrey's floppy hair seems to be doing a decent impersonation of the Elvis quiff all by itself.

With his face fixed into a perfect replica of Elvis's trademark sneer, he starts to sing: "Uhhh … I said one for the money …" His hips roll. His knees flick right and left. Pause. A chuckle or two emerge from the small audience.

"Two for the show …" His knees again flick left and right. Pause.

"Three to get ready now go cat go …" His "post-nuclear" arms now flap and flail in time with his legs, as he breaks into a full-on dance that appears plenty Elvis-like, but for the undersized arms fluttering as he moves.

Carrey brings "Blue Suede Shoes" to a big finish and drops to his knees. It is a dazzling early glimpse of the trademark physical comedy that he would go on to become known for.

Standing up, he regroups, grabbing a prop for his next bit. Carrey turns his back to the camera, putting on a fishing hat and a pair of big, wiry glasses, then turns back around again. He knits his eyebrows together, squints his eyes, and purses his lips, with the corners turned down in an expression of mournful suffering.

In an instant, he has transformed into Henry Fonda in his role as Norman Thayer, a curmudgeonly septuagenarian retired professor from the 1981 film *On Golden Pond*. He will soon shapeshift again into Katharine Hepburn, who plays Norman's loving wife, Ethel, as he plays both parts in the now-famous "strawberry scene."

Go pull the audition up on YouTube to get the full effect. It is truly a bravura (and at the same time, strange) performance, one that would become a defining moment of the "before they were famous" chapter of Carrey's career.

And it is a shining example of a moment where you can see someone's Blue Flame burning so brightly and vividly.

Even at this early age, Carrey was doing what he could do best, making great use of his signature talents: physicality, wit, expressiveness, and versatility. Case in point: he shifts seamlessly from Elvis to Henry Fonda to Katharine Hepburn in the span of two minutes.

And as is often the case with talent, Carrey's began to sprout early, watered by the environment in which he was raised.

"I watched the effect my father's love and humor had on the world around me, and I thought, 'That's something to do, that's something worth my time,' " Carrey reflected. "It wasn't long before I started acting up. People would come over to my house and they would be greeted by a seven-year-old throwing himself down a large flight of stairs. They would say, 'What happened?' And I would say, 'I don't know—let's check the replay.' And I would go back to the top of the stairs and come back down in slow motion."

Carrey could have chosen to put these budding talents to use in any of a number of ways, but he made a choice to use them to entertain people.

For much of Carrey's childhood, his mother was unwell. She had arthritis and phlebitis, and struggled with depression. The young Carrey loved his mom dearly, and like his father, dedicated himself to cheering her up. "I wanted her to be free. I wanted her to realize that her life was worth something because she gave birth to someone who was worth something."

Later in life, he better understood the higher calling—in Blue Flame language, the thing that he cared deeply about, or his purpose—that had drawn him down this path so early in life.

"When I was about 28, after a decade as a professional comedian, I realized one night in L.A. that the purpose of my life had always been to free people from concern, like my dad. When I realized this, I dubbed my new devotion, 'The Church of Freedom From Concern'—'The Church of FFC'—and I dedicated myself to that ministry."

This is what lit him up. Entertaining people in this way was not only invigorating in itself, but it was something he drew a great sense of meaning from.

This is the Blue Flame. It is the powerful intersection between *what you can do best, what you find most invigorating, and what you care deeply about.* Like Carrey, when you find the convergence of these three forces—your Blue Flame—you are then in a position to decide how to use it.

In a commencement address that Carrey delivered in 2014, he posed a question, the significance of which can't be overstated: "What's yours?" he asked, referring to the area where you can have the greatest impact. "How will you serve the world? What do they need that your talent can provide? That's all you have to figure out. As someone who has done what you are about to go do, I can tell you from experience, the effect you have on others is the most valuable currency there is."

Let me help bring this idea of the Blue Flame closer to home for you.

Think about that person in your organization who seems like they're totally rockin' it. With any luck, maybe that person is *you*.

They are doing the thing they were seemingly meant to be doing, playing in their proverbial "sweet spot." And it can be a beautiful thing to watch.

Now, imagine walking through the halls of your office and finding *everyone* in your company on fire in this way … in unison. It is a nirvana that leaders dream of achieving. What might a team or a company that is functioning at this high of a level be capable of?

What's more, imagine what would be possible if *you* were living in that same sweet spot. How would it turbocharge your effectiveness as a leader? How might it improve your life? How would it help you maximize your impact on your team and your company? On your family? On the world?

And, taking this line of thinking to its logical conclusion: Can you imagine what would be possible in a world where *all* people are acting, living, and working in alignment with their Blue Flame?

The goal of this book is to teach leaders everywhere this simple but powerful idea that has the power to tap into deep reservoirs of potential, motivation, and capability in others. In a world where leaders like you and me are always looking for an edge, the Blue Flame presents us with a real opportunity to get the best out of our people, and in doing so, propel our businesses to new heights.

These aren't empty clichés or pollyannaish self-help babble. I have seen the effect of the Blue Flame firsthand.

I have spent years working with growth-stage companies as an investor, executive, and coach, and have grown especially fascinated by the people in these companies who appear most *on fire*. People who are making big things happen, and who appear totally lit up while they're doing so. People who are having a huge impact in areas that matter to them. These are people whom you simply can't help but notice.

I wondered: What makes them tick? What makes them special? What kind of Wheaties do they eat for breakfast? And where can I get my hands on some of those?

> **How will you serve the world? What do they need that your talent can provide? That's all you have to figure out.**

The reality, of course, is that there isn't a single factor that drives human performance in the workplace. There is no secret ingredient or magic potion. And, despite the life-hacker headlines that try to convince you otherwise, there is no one key to success. I won't ever claim that the Blue Flame is a panacea, but in meticulously observing these stars—driven in part by my own fascination with human beings and what gets them firing—I noticed four things about them that seem to come up time and time again:

1. They seem to focus on what they can do best: They know their talents, have put in the hard work to cultivate those talents, and put them to good use.

2. They seem to have passion: A spark. A certain kind of energy. They have a clear sense of the types of activities they find energizing, and they try to focus their time, and talents, in these areas.

3. They seem to be inspired: They all find some level of purpose and meaning in the work they do. Something about it brings them deep and intrinsic satisfaction, which provides a potent and seemingly endless fuel source that powers early mornings, late nights, and intense workdays.

4. They seem to consciously use their talents, passions, and purpose in ways that can have great impact: They have figured out how to apply their talents, passions, and purpose to great effect within their companies. But many don't stop there. They use these same talents, passions, and purpose to have an impact within their families, communities, and the world at large.

In short, they've found and navigated toward something I later started to call their Blue Flame, which was an expanded take on an idea by the same name that

I learned about years back in a great book by Keith Ferrazzi, *Never Eat Alone*. In the book, Ferrazzi talks about the intersection of "talent and desire."

As growth-stage investors, my colleagues and I realized that working with leaders and teams who were playing in their Blue Flame wasn't just exciting to watch, but was absolutely vital to our success.

We reoriented our entire business toward putting *people* and their Blue Flames at the center of our strategy for success. Perhaps unsurprisingly, this simple idea—and all of the execution that was involved in incorporating the idea into our business model—has paid off in a big way in the form of outsized growth and above-market investment returns.

But this book isn't just about sharing these tried-and-true practices, and the brain science, organizational research, and anecdotes that support them. It is about something much bigger: inviting other leaders into this quest to bring this focus on *people*—and their talents, their passions, and their purpose—to the fore in American companies. It is about the far more universal idea that in a knowledge economy dependent on human capital, to achieve anything significant, our organizations need people who are on fire and burning blue.

WHY I WROTE THIS BOOK

As I discovered and brought this idea of the Blue Flame into the workplaces where I held leadership roles, its simplicity and usefulness quickly struck a chord with those on my teams. The idea of focusing on things that you can do best, that invigorate you, and that you care deeply about is rather uncontroversial, and quite commonsensical. But I soon realized that this idea resonated at a much deeper level, as it played to a few fundamental longings that most human beings in the workplace have: to be *seen* for their talents, to find their work energizing and *meaningful*, and to have *an impact* on their company and the world around them.

However, as I observed dozens of growth-stage companies over time, I noticed a disconnect: many workplaces aren't set up to encourage and foster this type of transformational Blue Flame leadership.

Though organizations generally recognize that helping people discover and lean into their talents, passions, and purpose is useful, many of them ultimately foster a culture that places greater value on the seemingly more important and urgent aspects of the business. The fires to put out. The monthly targets to hit. The deadlines to meet. After all these more pressing priorities, there isn't much room left to spend time on what one manager I worked with called "that fluffy people stuff." (Perhaps unsurprisingly, this manager's team was significantly underperforming.)

However, these urgent issues—while important by their very definition—can distract short-sighted leaders from the critically important, but oftentimes less-urgent focus on the most powerful growth lever they have in their business: their people.

I want to offer a simple and clarifying idea that can help leaders refocus their attention where it can have the most long-term impact.

At the most elemental level, businesses are nothing more than people working with other people to do stuff for more people.

People, it turns out, are the single most basic and important input to a business. In the same ways that "cells are the building blocks of a human life," humans are the fundamental building blocks of business. What else is there to a body than cells? In the same light, what else is there to an organization than people? (Okay ... and office space, paperclips, coffee makers, and the like, but you get the idea.)

In many organizations, responsibility for maximizing the return on a company's investment in personnel has been primarily assigned to the HR department. Many managers look to HR to roll out broad-based, programmatic performance management and talent development initiatives to help uplevel their people. They have abdicated their own responsibility in this area.

To illustrate, I once asked a manager in a new team I inherited why, based on an employee survey we commissioned, our employees were so thirsty for *mentorship and development*. "We've been waiting quarters for HR to roll something out, but it has never come!" the manager said. "You should ask them." This manager seemed to be missing a key point: that it is ultimately *our* responsibility as leaders to ensure that we are maximizing the impact that the talented humans we are leading are able to have.

I originally began writing this book to help change this paradigm in the companies that I worked with. To re-center managers at all levels of the organization on the performance-enhancing power of refocusing on *people*. And to equip them with the elemental-but-transformative idea of the Blue Flame—and the skills and confidence to have catalytic Blue Flame conversations. All as a means of helping them take their employees, and by extension their organization and companies, to new heights.

I taught this idea and method to other leaders in our organization, and they saw a similar impact.

People, it turns out, are the single most basic and important input to a business.

My original plan as I first put pen to paper was to draft up this concept for the purpose of sharing narrowly with the leaders in the organizations in which I worked. My hope was to use it to create a shared language and an enhanced way of leading within the team—one that stood for elevating and unleashing our people. It was to inspire them to lean into the power of Blue Flame leadership, which can be thrilling, rewarding, inspiring—and profitable. It was to create a mini-movement within our company around the idea of helping people discover their talents, their passions, and their purpose, and use these to have the greatest impact possible.

But I realized as I got into it that this idea—which I soon saw was abundant, limitless, and transcendent—shouldn't stay confined within the four walls of the companies I was working with. The world needed this now more than ever, and this idea needed to spread its wings. Its message was too important.

WHO THIS BOOK IS FOR

This book was designed to be a field guide for leaders who are looking for actionable, repeatable ways to get more out of their people and to deliver better results for their company. This includes:

- Leaders of growth-stage companies who are looking for an edge that can help them to unlock new levels of performance and growth.
- Leaders who want to spark and uplevel their teams, and help them deliver to their full potential.

- Leaders who want to make a lasting difference in the lives of those they lead.
- Leaders who also care about restoring humanity and human-centeredness in business.
- Anyone seeking a richer, more fulfilling, and more impactful life.

In the chapters that follow, we'll talk about why this concept is so important in today's knowledge economy, and we'll go on to cover each of the three components of the Blue Flame—helping your people find *what they're best at, what they find most invigorating,* and *what they care deeply about.* We will shorthand these as "talents," "passions," and "purpose," and look at each through the lenses of stories, research, brain science, and battle-tested firsthand experience.

Not only will I teach you how to use these ideas to elevate your leadership and ignite your team, but I will help you understand how to use these same ideas to look inward and discover your own Blue Flame. My hope is that in reading this book, you will uncover new facets of your own talents, passions, and purpose, and get in touch with new ways you can use those in your leadership at work, at home, in your community, and beyond.

The final chapter will provide a highly actionable playbook for using the ideas in this book to have transformative Blue Flame conversations with your team, peers, family, and other important people in your life.

On we go ...

CHAPTER 2

A New Kind of Fuel

> "Each of us has been made for some particular work, and the desire for that work has been put in every heart."
>
> — **Rumi**

The idea of the Blue Flame is not entirely a new concept. The Japanese have been talking about a similar idea dating back to the Heian period over a thousand years ago. They call it Ikigai (pronounced eek-ee-guy), which roughly translates to "a life worth living."

It is the reason you get up in the morning. It is what gets and keeps you going, similar to the raison d'être in French culture. And it is a maxim, a way of life, to the long-lived residents of Okinawa, the largest in a chain of islands in the East China Sea, south of Tokyo.

The female population of Okinawa boasts the longest life expectancy of anyone anywhere in the world. There are five times more female centenarians per 100,000 in Okinawa than there are in the United States. The incidence of breast cancer, colon cancer, and cardiovascular disease among women in Okinawa is one-fifth that of their American counterparts.

They eat well, and moderately. They lead active lifestyles. They have strong and rich social connections. And they grow up steeped in the ancient philosophy of Ikigai.

Ikigai gives Okinawa residents what Dan Buettner, author of *Blue Zones*, calls "a vocabulary for a sense of purpose."[1] That is: knowing what you are living for.

What is it exactly? Japanese scientist Ken Mogi put it simply, "If you can find pleasure and satisfaction in what you do and you're good at it, congratulations, you have found your Ikigai."[2]

---

[1] Dan Buettner, "How to Live to Be 100+," TED Talk, September 2009, https://www.ted.com/talks/dan_buettner_how_to_live_to_be_100.
[2] Lucy Dayman, "Ikigai: The Japanese Concept of Finding Purpose in Life," Savvy Tokyo, January 15, 2020, https://savvytokyo.com/ikigai-japanese-concept-finding-purpose-life/.

Ikigai isn't just a momentary self-help technique. It is an enduring way of living for Okinawans. The vibrant centenarians of Okinawa keep doing what lights their fire, even in their old age. A 100-year-old fisherman goes out fishing three times a week to put food on the table for his family because he is good at it, and it is what has given him a sense of satisfaction and purpose throughout his life. A 102-year-old woman finds a deep sense of meaning in looking after her great-great-great-granddaughter.

The concept of Ikigai has been represented graphically as the intersection of *four* essential questions about life:

- What do you love—what makes you come alive?
- What are you great at?
- What do you most want to achieve or make happen?
- What do people value about what you do—how can you be most useful?

But as central as this idea is to the Japanese way of life, it has not made it across the pond to Western culture in the same way, let alone into American workplaces.

We're missing out.

Unlike the Japanese fisherman whose work brings him a deep sense of fulfillment and pleasure, there is a large contingent of American workers who punch in in the morning, and start counting the hours until the clock strikes 5:00 p.m. Some are sufficiently effective in their jobs (others less so), but as they apathetically trudge through the day, you can't help but wonder how much more they have to give that their company, and the world, simply isn't seeing.

Let's nonjudgmentally shorthand this segment of our workforce as the "PIPOs" (the "punch-in, punch-out" types). They are the uninspired among us who haven't yet found their Blue Flame. They go through their working years collecting a paycheck, and counting the days until retirement. Their work drains them, instead of filling them up. Their job is just a job.

At one time or another, many of us will feel PIPO-ish ourselves, whether it is as a result of being in the wrong job, failing to see the impact of the work that we do, having an uninspiring boss, working in a disheartening or hostile work environment, or just feeling stuck. I've certainly been there.

The cult-classic movie *Office Space* gives us a satirical window into life in a soul-sucking, uninspiring, fluorescent-lit workplace in mid-1990s corporate America. The staff at the fictional tech company, Initech, are almost all PIPOs, oozing indifference, active disgruntledness, or downright anger. The movie casts a light on the most dreaded aspects of American office life: jargon-filled memos, awkward office parties, and uninspiring leadership, to name a few.

Office Space was inspired by the stereotype of the uninspiring American workplace, known for its focus on conformity, top-down leadership, needless bureaucracy, and general malaise.

The main character, Peter Gibbons, laments to his girlfriend, Joanna, "I don't know why I can't just go to work and be happy."

"Peter," Joanna says matter of factly, "most people don't like their jobs."

Thankfully, it seems that American corporate culture has taken steps forward since the late-1990s. The command-and-control style of micromanaging that Initech's cringeworthy boss Bill Lumbergh so epitomized has been broadly recognized as being less effective than more empowering leadership (although there are still plenty of Lumbergh-types running around American workplaces today). Ideas like "conscious capitalism" and "purpose-driven business" have come further to the fore. Companies have also recognized that the work environment has a big impact on workers' overall happiness and productivity. This is why windowless, cubicle-filled offices have begun to make way for vibrantly colored, ping-pong-table-adorned open workspaces.

But Joanna's assertion that "most people don't like their jobs" has proven timeless, as the data today shows that Americans' satisfaction with their work hasn't improved much since the '90s. Why is this? Well, it turns out that it takes more than a casual dress code, kombucha, and some beanbag chairs to help workers come alive.

In the early 1970s, oil consumption was on the rise in America. Industrialization was continuing to drive rapidly increasing energy use in the commercial sector. More and more Americans were cruising around in their sleek Ford Pintos, clad in tunic tops and bell bottoms, and a freshly done-up perm or mullet.

But an oil embargo imposed by OPEC in 1973 wreaked havoc on global supply, which led to fuel shortages and sky-high energy prices.

It takes more than a casual dress code, kombucha, and some beanbag chairs to help workers come alive.

With prices at the pump skyrocketing, Johnny and Jenny McCool all of a sudden had to find Friday night plans other than cruising the local strip in their Pinto. What's more, the massive spike in oil prices sent shock waves through the American economy, as energy produced by oil was among the most significant resources powering our industrial sector.

The short-term effects were painful, and lingered through the end of the decade. But long-term, the crisis was a huge blow to the American automotive sector, as it shifted the advantage toward Japanese manufacturers who had been producing smaller, more fuel-efficient vehicles.

Oil was the fuel that the global economy ran on. And in many ways, it still is today.

But fast-forward nearly half a century, and while our economy is still reliant on oil, we find ourselves in a new era in American commerce. It is one where information, skills, and motivation have begun to supersede raw materials, capital equipment, and energy as the primary inputs that power the so-called knowledge economy. It is an era when human, intellectual, and informational capital are the primary fuel source driving economic growth.

Against the backdrop of this *knowledge economy*, we are in the midst of a different type of energy crisis right now, one that has been playing out beneath our noses, and that many American companies have overlooked.

Imagine, for a moment, that we have access to a brand-new source of free, clean energy. There are nearly limitless reserves of it at our disposal, but we haven't yet chosen to throw the switch and power up our organizations with this new energy.

In a competitive world in which companies face finite resources and are constantly seeking an edge, why would we not endeavor to do that?

It turns out there are deep reservoirs of this stuff that we have yet to drill into. And unlike the oil crisis of the industrial era in the 1970s, American companies aren't at the mercy of expensive oil and gas exploration projects, or volatile energy prices to tap into it. This fuel is virtually free, and it sits in the hearts and minds of our people.

AN ENERGY CRISIS IN THE KNOWLEDGE ECONOMY

Leaders like you and me are the ignition switches that can activate the untapped energy of employees who are not fully engaged with the work they do. We have a chance to build organizations that are full to the brim with talented, passionate, and purposeful team members, and in doing so, light up our companies' power grids.

But today, the average company's power grid is sputtering. Some are dealing with full-on rolling blackouts.

Around the time that *Office Space* was released, Gallup, the consulting and analytics company, began publishing a national employee engagement index. To date, they have collected information from almost 31 million employees. In their 2018 *State of the American Workplace* survey, they found that only 34 percent of American workers identified as "engaged" in their jobs, up modestly from 26 percent in 2000. That means for at least the past twenty years, we have managed to truly engage only about a third of our workforce.

We are in the midst of a different type of energy crisis right now, one that has been playing out beneath our noses.

This is not what I would call fuel-efficient. For growth-stage companies, this might feel like trying to drive a Lamborghini that is outfitted with a 20-horsepower go-kart engine.

The same survey found that 13 percent of US employees were "actively disengaged." These workers are outright unhappy and, at worst, feel hostility toward their workplace. As a result, they tend to upset customers, drag down coworkers, and dilute or undermine the good work of their more engaged colleagues.

The remaining 53 percent are "not engaged." These are the PIPOs and Peter Gibbonses of the world. They punch in, lunch pail in hand, go through the motions with one eye on the clock, then punch out at the end of the day. Rinse and repeat, day after day. Many of them try—they really do—but they find it tough to stay motivated to give their best. As a result, their employers aren't getting their best.

As the Gallup survey puts it, "They may be generally satisfied but are not cognitively and emotionally connected to their work and workplace."[3]

Understanding this troubling reality left me with the unshakable feeling that there has to be a better way. And so began my quest to understand the root of this stubbornly persistent challenge facing leaders and their companies.

THE FISH STINKS FROM THE HEAD

My quest to understand why such a large chunk of our working population is unengaged led me through reams of organizational, psychological, and neurological research, and to the doorsteps of talented leaders and organizational and developmental psychologists.

At the same time, within my day job as an executive leader in growth-stage companies, I was having dozens of what I would later call "Blue Flame conversations" with the people on my teams.

I came to learn that these conversations were really important to helping me get the best stuff that these talented people had to give. It enabled me to help teammates pivot out of jobs where they were struggling and into roles where they would crush it. It allowed me to help them reconnect with the reason they entered their line of work in the first place. With remarkable consistency, I saw individual and team performance strengthen as a result.

As I proceeded down these two parallel paths of research and on-the-job practice, the dots started to connect between the two. I grew increasingly convinced that the transformative impact of Blue Flame leadership that I have witnessed in the trenches as a leader could play a big role in helping to breathe life back into the stubbornly disengaged population within the American workforce.

---

[3] Jim Harter, "Employee Engagement on the Rise in the U.S.," Gallup.com, August 26, 2018, https://news.gallup.com/poll/241649/employee-engagement-rise.aspx.

The workplace has the potential to be a place of incredible fulfillment and growth in our lives; or, like the fictional Initech of *Office Space*, it has the possibility of becoming a black hole where passions, talents, and potential go to get sucked in and swallowed up, never to be seen again.

The difference comes down to leadership. Good ol' fashioned leadership.

They say when an organization is rotten—like Initech—*the fish stinks from the head*. This means the leadership has created an environment in which both employees and, by extension, the organization itself suffer.

As leaders, it is our *choice* whether we will use our role and responsibility as a platform from which to elicit the best in our people, and in doing so, help them come alive. Or whether we will instead perpetuate the troubling status quo.

Through this lens, leadership isn't a title, but a stewardship. We have a responsibility—to our people, to our companies, and (if you choose) to the world—to band together and help people find deeper fulfillment in their work.

This is important not only because it is the right thing to do for the teammates who spend 40 percent of their waking hours supporting your company's mission, but it is critical if you want to be successful as a business.

SHOW ME THE MONEY

In a world of growing complexity, I've learned that sometimes the simplest ideas like this can be the most impactful. And leadership—as a discipline, a skill, and a way of being—is in desperate need of a "return to simplicity."

Amazon lists over 40,000 titles under the subject of "leadership," each with its own take, its own model, its own "15 keys to leadership success." I'll even admit to having my own self-limiting beliefs as to whether the world needed yet another leadership book called *The Blue Flame*.

But as valuable as many of these books are, these 15-principle leadership models can sometimes run the risk of confusing a really essential point: *at its very core, a leader's role is to cultivate and grow the talent and passion of their people, and put people into positions where they can apply that talent and passion in the ways that can have the greatest impact on their shared mission.*

In a world plagued by scarcity thinking and littered with zero-sum equations, putting our people into a position where they can use their talent, do things that they find invigorating, and discover meaning in their work can yield one of those abundant "everybody wins" scenarios. Employees are able to feel more fulfilled and be more effective and impactful. Their coworkers feel the positive ripple effect of this and draw inspiration. And companies like yours—and your shareholders—get the benefit of higher performance.

For those of you saying, "Yeah, yeah, yeah, Dan. I get the fluffy 'make lives better' stuff, but you need to tell me how this will make my business more successful! Show me the money!" the evidence that Blue Flame thinking can translate into real business results is out there, and it is truly eye-opening.

Gallup's survey and other studies help us understand what this can mean for companies like yours. Gallup set out its own definition of 'business success,' which is based on a combination of various metrics: financial results; customer satisfaction; staff retention; quality of goods and services produced; shrinkage (theft); and absenteeism. Big picture, businesses or work units that scored in the top quartile for employee engagement have nearly double the odds of success compared to those in the lowest percentile. The organizations in the 99th percentile have four times the success rate of those in the 1st percentile. *When people are meaningfully engaged it's a triple win: teammates win, the team wins, companies win.*

In more direct terms, the businesses in the top quartile, when compared with those in the bottom quartile, experienced 17 percent higher productivity. They also have 10 percent higher customer metrics, 41 percent lower absenteeism, 70 percent fewer employee safety incidents, 20 percent higher sales, and 21 percent higher profitability, compared with organizations with the lowest employee engagement.

Thinking about this in terms of the direct and quantifiable impact it can have on your business is exciting. But as corporate citizens, it is important to also look at the bird's-eye view of what this can mean for our country.

Gallup reports that there were, in round numbers, about 100 million full-time US employees at the time of their most recent survey, and that a total of 66 percent were either "not engaged" or "actively disengaged."

That's 66 percent of 100 million US full-time employees. Let's pencil out the math. Luckily, it's an easy one, even for me.

The workplace has the potential to be a place of incredible fulfillment and growth in our lives; or, like the fictional Initech of *Office Space*, it has the possibility of becoming a black hole where passions, talents, and potential go to get sucked in and swallowed up, never to be seen again.

This means there are 66 million people in the US who are not "actively engaged" in their work. That's just a fraction less than the populations of the two most populous US states—California (39.5 million) and Texas (29 million)—squished together.

Try to imagine what would happen to the economy if every man, woman, child, and baby in the states of California and Texas were employed in US industry and had suddenly come alive and started burning blue. (Yeah, I know about employment and child labor laws. But you get the idea.)

To look at it from the opposite angle, let's examine the wasted productivity. GDP in the US is forecast to reach around $22 trillion in 2020. That means that every 1 percent increase in productivity generates an additional $220 billion per year.

And Gallup shows that the companies in the top quartile in terms of engagement are 17 percent more productive than those in the fourth quartile. So by extension, if we were able to get that fourth quartile humming in the same way that the first quartile is, there are several trillion dollars of economic gain to be had. More than the market cap of Microsoft and Apple—combined. These are not small potatoes.

The figures are even more alarming—and exciting—as you look at the data on a global level, but I think you get the point: the scale of the global economic potential leaking out of the bottom of the bucket because we are failing to light our people up is colossal.

THE RETURN ON CULTURE

The companies that are getting this right are getting it very right, and reaping the benefits.

Hilton, a global leader in hospitality with over six thousand properties across fifteen well-known hotel brands, topped the 2020 US ranking of the *Fortune 100 Best Companies to Work For* for the second year running. It is the only non-tech company to have achieved this feat, and the only hospitality company to have reached the number one spot.

The Hilton San Diego Bayfront one of my personal favorite Hilton properties, is perched on the shore of the San Diego Bay, an inlet on the southern California coast that creates a natural deep-water harbor. From the terrace of the hotel's Odysea Bar there are stunning views across to the Silver Strand, the sandy isthmus that separates the harbor from the Pacific Ocean.

At the bar of the Odysea, a thick-set, sandy-haired man is fixing cocktails. He seems a little older than the other staff. As he mixes the bar's trademark Odysea Mule (vodka, St-Germain liqueur, lime, angostura, ginger beer, since you asked), he chats with the customers, and apologizes if he's slow. It's his first day. He offers the cocktail to the customer and urges him to try it first. "If it's not perfect, Antonio will fix you one. He's the cocktail genius." The customer makes a big show of trying the drink. "It's perfect!" he announces, laughing. The bartender grins happily and turns to the next customer. "Hi there! What can I get you?"

The evidence that Blue Flame thinking can translate into real business results is out there, and it is truly eye-opening.

This particular bartender is having a challenging week because, well, he isn't actually a bartender. Yesterday he was working laundry, the day before he was a bellman, tomorrow he's on the front desk checking in guests and handling guest issues, and the next day he'll be cleaning rooms and joining engineers on service calls. He is one of Hilton's senior executives and is taking part in the hotel group's immersion program where executives spend a week working on the front lines of the operations, meeting team members and customers, and experiencing firsthand the day-to-day challenges and opportunities that team members face.

Flattening the org chart in this way—working to minimize the distance between management and the frontline staff that make the company tick—has become a hallmark of Hilton culture.

As is the case with many companies, Hilton's culture was shaped around the values of its founder, Conrad Hilton.

Hilton founded his namesake hotel brand in 1919 when he bought his first hotel in Cisco, Texas, and slowly and methodically built the brand over several decades. Fast-forward some time later to the 1950s and Hilton had become a nationally recognized brand.

In his 1957 book, *Be My Guest,* Hilton details the ten keys to success upon which he built the brand. Number one on his list is: *Find Your Own Particular Talent.*

Conrad Hilton was a big believer in the idea that each person has the ability to be great at something, and should find, nurture, and lean into that thing (sound familiar?), and built Hilton's culture around this premise.

"Finding this particular talent is the first step in the art of successful living. ... Don't worry if it takes a little time to find your own niche. This is no invitation to become a drifter, a professional malcontent. But every man has a right, a duty I would say, to search humbly and prayerfully for the place where he fits into the divine pattern."

It is no wonder that the company has been a perennial best place to work. It is a culture that focuses first on its people and creating an environment where they can find, develop, and apply their talents; one that encourages its employees to "dream big," one that promotes enthusiasm and positivity, and one that "looks down to no one"—each a tenet of Conrad Hilton's early philosophy.

Today, Hilton's Chief Human Resources Officer Matthew Schuyler characterizes Hilton as a business of *"people serving people."* "For the longest time," he says, "one of [Hilton's] greatest learnings has been to harness the energy of a collective purpose among those people. People want to come to work because it will bring them meaning."

This philosophy is especially important in the hospitality industry, where the interaction between frontline staff and customers plays a large part in defining the customer experience and, by extension, whether customers return. Hilton's success hinges upon these everyday interactions between team members and guests. When its team members are enveloped in a culture that takes care of and celebrates its people, the guests can surely feel it.

Sure, if it is near-term productivity they were solving for, then Hilton's leadership team would probably think differently about sending their executives to make mai tais or fluff pillows for a week. But they can see the bigger picture: leaders who are attuned to what their employees and customers are experiencing day-to-day are going to be in a much better position to cultivate a culture that can bring the best out of its people. And its customers expect the best out of the company's frontline people.

Hilton has also created numerous programs that support its US hotel and corporate team members in pursuing their unique professional and personal career aspirations. Its Thrive Sabbatical Program offers employees four weeks off and $5,000 to pursue a personal goal.

As Schuyler says, "Give humans a chance to be great, and they will generally be great, and so that's really our model with respect to [creating] career opportunities."[4]

It is no wonder that in 2019, Hilton had nearly 1.35 million job applicants in the US, an average of twenty-six applications per vacancy.

Unsurprisingly, at the time this book was written, Hilton was outperforming its peer set (other large publicly traded hotel operators) and significantly outperforming the S&P 500 index.

As Hilton's success demonstrates, when we engage the talented people within our organizations, when we light them up with purpose and allow them to do what they do best, when we help them find their own Blue Flame, it is possible to unleash huge amounts of human energy into a company's power grid. For free.

---

[4] "Why Hilton Is the Best Company to Work For in America," Great Place to Work, accessed July 10, 2020, https://www.greatplacetowork.com/resources/podcast/why-hilton-is-the-best-company-to-work-for-in-america.

THE TOLL ON AMERICAN WORKERS

With all this talk about the cold, hard financial benefits of lighting our people up, it is important to remember that the importance of the Blue Flame extends beyond the dollars and cents, beyond the financial payoff. For some of our trusted teammates out there, finding a greater sense of fulfillment and satisfaction in their work could also be a matter of life or death.

In his most recent book, *Dying for a Paycheck*, Stanford professor Jeffrey Pfeffer—a prolific writer and one of the country's leading business thinkers—concluded that "workplace environments in the United States may be responsible for 120 thousand excess deaths per year."

Pfeffer compares the effects of bad workplace practices as being "as harmful to health ... as exposure to secondhand smoke." Pfeffer's conclusion applies not only to physically dangerous work environments, like operating heavy machinery or running a grizzly bear breeding operation; his research covers companies of all kinds, across sectors.

> **Give humans a chance to be great, and they will generally be great.**

In 2015, Bank of America intern Moritz Erhardt was days away from being offered a full-time job at the bank's London office. Breaking into investment banking at a prominent firm like Bank of America is a defining moment for an aspiring finance professional like Moritz, and he deserved it. He had been putting in remarkably long hours to prove he had what it takes to succeed in the fast-paced, cutthroat, and highly lucrative environment.

But Erhardt didn't live to receive his offer letter. He was found dead in a shower at his London apartment after working seventy-two hours in a row under intense, stressful conditions. He suffered an epileptic fit that many assume was triggered by exhaustion.[5]

In response to stressful situations, the body releases the hormone cortisol. This system is designed to give us a quick boost of energy to deal with an immediate threat—a shadowy figure walking toward you in an alley, or a spouse reaching to

---

[5] David Jones, "Bank of America Intern: Was Moritz Erhardt Killed by His Ambition to Match High Flying Father?," *Daily Mail Online*, August 23, 2013, https://www.dailymail.co.uk/news/article-2401220/Bank-America-intern-Moritz-Erhardt-killed-ambition-match-high-flying-father.html.

grab the last slice of pizza without asking. But when cortisol levels remain high over long periods of time, it can result in inflammation, heart disease, and accelerated cell death, contributors to a whole host of nasty health issues.

In its thirteenth annual *Stress in America* survey, the American Psychological Association reported that work is the most significant stressor in people's lives. Over 60 percent of people report work as their number one stressor. Money—which isn't altogether separate from work—claims second place.

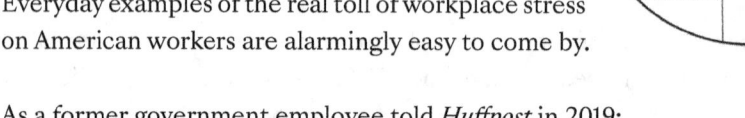

Everyday examples of the real toll of workplace stress on American workers are alarmingly easy to come by.

As a former government employee told *Huffpost* in 2019:

> "I loved my work, but hated going each day because of [my supervisor]. I would get physically ill knowing when she would be around. Emails from her would give me serious anxiety and hives. If she requested meetings, I would have stress attacks and cold sweats. I didn't sleep, constantly worrying about work—and was ill frequently. I ended up in the ICU at 36 [years old] and had serious work-induced anxiety."[6]

Over 60 percent of people report work as their number one stressor.

In another instance, Paula Davis-Laack, a successful lawyer, left her job to spread awareness about early-career burnout. She founded the Stress & Resilience Institute, which educates people about chronic exhaustion, creeping cynicism, disconnection from other people, loss of confidence, and other classic symptoms of stress-related burnout. Reflecting on her own experience with workplace stress, she writes:

> "Getting out of bed to go to work had become exceedingly difficult, if not emotionally painful. My pop out of bed, ready to start the week, had become a slow drop and thud. Weekends weren't long enough to fully recover (even when I didn't work), and vacations, when I actually took them, provided only temporary relief. Every work or life curveball, no matter how minor,

---

[6] Monica Torres, "8 Times People Hated a Job So Much It Made Them Ill," *HuffPost*, January 28, 2019, https://www.huffingtonpost.co.uk/entry/hate-job-stress-feels-like_l_5c4a07b2e4b0e1872d4213a3

became a major deal. I remember my mom calling and asking me to pick up some groceries on my way out to her house, and I had a level 10 reaction to her very basic request. That was not my personality, and it was a red flag."[7]

The stress epidemic comes with its own financial burden, imposing yet another tax on American businesses. The American Institute of Stress estimates that stress-related accidents; absenteeism; employee turnover; lost productivity; direct medical, legal, and insurance fees; and compensation awards cost US businesses over $300 billion per year.

In his book, Pfeffer comes to a straightforward conclusion: "Any workplace practice that increases stress makes human well-being worse and health-care costs higher, while any management practice that either directly mitigates stress or provides ways of coping with it increases well-being and reduces health-care costs correspondingly."

FROM STRESS TO EXHILARATION

We need to remember that as leaders, when people come to work for us, they have placed their physical and psychological well-being in our hands.

But with all of this doom and gloom about the toll that stress and disengaging work is having on American workers, what can we do about it?

Stress is unavoidable, right?

"The workplace is stressful because it's tough out there," you might say. "We have competitors who are trying to steal the bread from our table," you might tell me. "You can't ask business leaders to take their foot off the gas. Work should be challenging, and stress is inevitable. Suck it up!"

And it is true that staying ahead in an increasingly competitive global economy isn't easy. As a fellow business leader like you, I understand this firsthand.

Work is supposed to be challenging, but if we let ourselves believe that degradation of mental or physical health is just an unavoidable byproduct of challenging work, we have totally missed the point.

---

[7] Paula Davis-Laack, "I Fought the Law and the Law Won: My Burnout Story," The Stress & Resilience Institute, January 16, 2020, https://stressandresilience.com/my-burnout-story/.

Any company that is endeavoring to do something challenging and worthwhile needs its people to bring their best stuff each day. And stress and disengagement are massive barriers that stand in the way of getting the best out of people.

But when leaders focus on helping their people to discover and lean into their Blue Flames, the demands of difficult work—even severe demands—become just challenges. And challenges can be exciting and surmountable when we are approaching them from our zone of talent, passion, and purpose.

When leaders embrace the idea of the Blue Flame, an important shift is possible. We can move from the burden and downside of *stress* to the activating feeling of *exhilaration*.

Ask a passionate and talented composer if writing their latest score was stressful. Ask the same question of a mountaineer about his last summit, or a painter about their last work of art. My guess is they might look a little confused.

"Er, it was challenging at times, but I got satisfaction from overcoming those challenges. Actually, it was exhilarating. I wouldn't get any satisfaction if it wasn't hard work. The hard work and the challenges are what bring meaning to my life because I like what I am doing. I'm good at it. And it has meaning to me."

★ ★ ★

By now, you are probably thinking, "Wait, so Dan, you're telling me that I can reduce my costs, improve my sales, help my employees find more fulfillment and satisfaction in their work, and help them live a healthier life? All at the same time?" You summarized it well, although it sounded a bit like an infomercial when you said it like that. The bottom line is that while helping our teammates find and lean into their Blue Flame may not be a panacea, it can go a long way toward helping to deliver the things that leaders like you have been entrusted with delivering, namely *results*.

IN CASE YOU MISSED IT: THE KEY IDEAS

A New Kind of Fuel: Move over, crude oil. Today's knowledge economy is operating on an entirely different type of energy: the talents, passions, and motivation of human beings. We live in an era when human and intellectual capital are the primary fuel source driving economic growth. There are deep reservoirs of this stuff within our people, but most companies are tapping into only a fraction of it.

Today's Energy Crisis: A full 66 percent of American workers rate themselves as unengaged at work, and the cost is significant. The low productivity, higher absenteeism, and greater workplace stress among this population is imposing a significant invisible tax on companies, and harming employee well-being.

A Significant and Grave Cost: Disengagement costs the American economy trillions of dollars in lost productivity each year. But what's even more alarming is that the workplace stress that many within this disengaged population experience is responsible for up to 120,000 excess deaths per year.

The Ping-Pong Table Myth: Just because your office offers free kombucha and an in-office masseuse does not mean everyone can suddenly become happy and stress-free. These sorts of perks are well-intentioned, but merely bandages over deeper challenges.

But There's Hope: When people are engaged by their work and feel empowered by their leaders, otherwise stressful work can become exhilarating and invigorating. And it pays. Organizations with higher employee engagement enjoy significantly better financial performance, whereas organizations with lower employee engagement suffer poorer performance and less growth.

It Comes Down to Leadership: When leaders like you put more emphasis on helping their employees discover and lean into their Blue Flames, not only can it help mitigate the substantial cost of disengagement and workplace stress, but it can help create the rare but powerful "triple win"—employees win, teams win, and the company wins.

CHAPTER 3

"This Could Change Everything"

My own journey with Blue Flame leadership began in the whitewashed halls of finance, a sector usually not mentioned in the same paragraph as the words *passion* and *engagement*.

I have spent over a decade working with Alpine Investors, a San Francisco-based private equity group that invests in mid-sized growth-stage companies across the US. The firm has had extraordinary success on the back of a simple but powerful principle: the key to success in growing companies comes down to *working with, learning from, and developing great people.*

We held a view that when you strip a company down to the studs, the most elemental resource that comprises it—and every business—is people. Real, human, people.

A while back, we had a seemingly obvious realization that changed the trajectory of our firm forever: simply put, our success was dependent on *people*. This people-first perspective is one that we came to learn was rather unique in the world of finance, an industry where our training taught us that success was driven by discounted cash flow models, total addressable market sizes, and EBITDA multiples.

Important as these technical elements are, the lightbulb moment came when we observed that within the companies where we had leadership teams whose talents were aligned with the needs of the roles they were charged with playing, and who were aligned behind a compelling and motivating purpose and vision, we were having success. And in situations where one of those two things were missing, we were seeing considerably less success.

When you strip a company down to the studs, the most elemental resource that comprises it—and every business—is people.

This led us to ponder: *If the presence of talented, purpose-driven teams is highly correlated with our success, then what if we designed our business and our growth strategy around putting people at the heart of it all? What if we became black belts at unleashing great people into high-potential companies, and putting these people into roles where they do what they do best? What if we could help immerse them in a culture that lights them up and inspires them to bring their best every day?*

As an investment firm, we continued to hold an appreciation for the non-people elements of intelligent investing: the "technicals" like making sure our well-tuned discounted cash flow analysis supported the purchase price we were willing to pay. But in a crowded private equity market, we found a wide-open playing field in a new kind of investing in *people*.

Here is the essence of our formula:

- Invest in high-quality, high-potential businesses
- Ensure that they are chock-full of great, value-aligned people who are in roles that leverage their greatest talents, passions, and purpose—that ignite their Blue Flames.
- Help these people to get aligned behind a soulful purpose, a bold and purposeful vision for their company, and a winning strategy.
- Support these people with development, mentorship, training, connections, perspective, and resources (including capital).
- Watch these people and their companies soar.

This strategy, dubbed "People First," has undeniably worked, as measured by investment returns that have been consistently and materially above market.

Along the way, I have had a front-row seat to the common challenges, issues, and opportunities growth-stage companies face, and I have noticed a number of common themes that led me to believe in the importance of writing this book.

Observation #1: Putting people first in this way isn't common, and non-believers are leaving a lot on the table as a result.
It isn't that these companies don't employ talented people—remember: *all people have talents*—nor is it that leadership is too dense to see that people matter to their company's success.

Instead, I've observed that many small to mid-sized companies (and even some large ones) don't prioritize finding, recruiting, and lighting up talented people because of all of the competing important-and-urgent demands of running a small, resource-constrained company. This tends to show up in slipshod hiring practices that lead to low hiring success rates, low employee engagement scores, and high turnover rates.

Companies that don't prioritize lighting their people up are leaving a lot on the table as a result.

Unsurprisingly, as we discussed last chapter there's a tight correlation between the degree to which companies invest in bringing the best out of their people and real hard-dollar results. Remember the statistics from earlier that suggest that organizations with the highest employee engagement have 20 percent higher sales and 21 percent higher profitability (when compared with organizations with the lowest employee engagement)?

In 2019, *USA Today* studied employee-review website Glassdoor to uncover both the best and worst companies to work for according to their employees.

At the time, the average employee rating for the thousands of companies listed on Glassdoor was 3.4 out of 5. Connecticut-based cable and internet supplier Frontier Communications held the second lowest score of any organization listed, coming in at a paltry 2.5 out of 5. Grocery chain the Fresh Market took the booby prize with a rating of 2.4. It should be noted that Bill Lumbergh's (fictional) Initech managed to elude the *USA Today* shit list.

Only 28 percent of Frontier employees said they would "recommend Frontier to a friend as a place of employment" and only 22 percent approved of the then-CEO (who stepped down in December 2019). The newspaper's probe into Glassdoor reviews of the company revealed that employees commonly cite "a negative culture and poor relations with senior management."

The reviews don't make for happy reading:

- *"Lack of management, average pay, if you have no seniority you aren't going to have a good time."*
- *"Unattainable numbers, untrained reps, outsourced, horrible service all around, high school clique, HORRIBLE, extreme stress, just horrible."*
- *"Management were all hired through nepotism so none of them know the job at all, creating an environment where management asks for the world."*

Uncoincidentally, Frontier's share price plummeted by more than 50 percent year over year.

Now it has to be said that Frontier has faced some very real ongoing business issues. The company faced major challenges integrating various assets acquired from Verizon and AT&T some years back, leading to unhappy customers and an exodus of broadband subscribers; this on top of the more secular "cord cutting" trend that has weighed on the sector (and will continue to).

Companies that don't prioritize lighting their people up are leaving a lot on the table.

But when your employees are telling you loud and clear that they are not enjoying the experience of working for your organization, it means the problem lies deeper than market conditions.

By contrast, the current "best place to work in the United States," according to Glassdoor ratings, is sales and marketing software developer HubSpot, whose employee rate the company 4.6 out of 5 overall.

Ninety-six percent of employees would recommend them as a place of work and 98 percent approve of the CEO and cofounder, Brian Halligan.

Here are some of the things employees say about HubSpot:

- *"Excellent people, good culture, treat employees well."*
- *"I am constantly amazed by our executive leadership team and how they care for and prioritize our employees"*
- *"You really have a lot of autonomy in the work you do."*
- *"Smart, helpful and friendly coworkers. Small teams grant tons of autonomy with very low process/meeting burden."*
- *"Fantastic company to work in, with attentive managers and fantastic, diverse and inclusive culture."*
- *"Steady leadership that responds well to criticism and knows when to make changes."*
- *"Everybody is genuinely committed to HubSpot values. Culture, values, and mission are real, not only words written somewhere."*

Naturally, some slim portion of their employees don't share such glowing reviews, but I think you catch the drift: employees generally dig working there.

Uncoincidentally, HubSpot's revenue for the year prior saw a near 32 percent increase year-over-year, and the company has outperformed the S&P 500 nearly tenfold from 2016 to 2019.

The data is clear: if your employees are motivated and encouraged to use their talents, it is far more likely that your bottom line is happy.

Observation #2: The impact of helping people to uncover and work in alignment with their Blue Flame can be significant.
Teams of people operating in their Blue Flame feed on each other, and work becomes invigorating rather than draining. When surrounded by the right set of conditions, they get into a state of group flow that can feel intoxicating. Their companies' bottom lines see the impact.

The process starts with helping those we lead develop a clear sense of their Blue Flame, something that surprisingly few people have a well-developed perspective on.

In one instance, I inherited a team headed by a talented leader we'll call Sandra. She had been with the company for years and was one of those lifer types who knew the company inside and out. She knew where every paper clip was stored, recalled every individual customer ID number by heart, and remembered the name of every employee's spouse.

Like each of us, Sandra had a distinct set of talents that distinguished her from those around her. She was meticulous—no "t" would go uncrossed on her watch. She was also unrelenting in her follow-through—nothing would slip between the cracks when Sandra was in charge. She was a strong executor, a disciplined and systematic taskmaster, and if you gave her a playbook to run, she'd run it like a finely tuned engine.

At the time, the challenge that our organization faced was that the customer service department that she was leading needed to undergo significant transformation in order to support our company's vision of providing the easiest, most enjoyable, and most digitally powered customer experience. As our company entered a new phase of growth, we needed to re-architect customer service to be more proactive, scalable, and technology-enabled.

This change would require leadership that could see around corners to understand how customer service needs were evolving. The change would require breaking from our current thinking about what customer service is and completely rethinking and redesigning our service model in order to remain competitive in our market. It was a classic case of, "What got us here won't get us there."

The type of leadership needed in this next chapter of growth and scaling was different from what was needed in prior eras, where success was dependent upon strong execution of the playbook we had—an area in which Sandra had proven herself to be especially effective.

In the customer service leadership post she occupied, we needed vision. We needed a strong attunement to and deep empathy for the evolving needs of our customers. We needed an architect's mind.

As this mission came into view, it grew clear that there was a growing gap between Sandra's talents and the new mandate. She tried hard to lean into the new needs of the role, embracing coaching and support along the way, but it was evident that building and using these new muscles wasn't coming naturally.

This is a critical moment that many leaders face; there comes a time when you realize that the signature talents your team member possesses aren't perfectly aligned with those needed to thrive in the role they are in.

Leaders in this situation find themselves with a few options. On the one hand, you can hope that they'll raise their game and rise to the challenge—and in some cases, depending on the degree and nature of the talent mismatch, that gap can be closed with training, coaching, and support.

Alternatively, you can pair them with someone who complements them in the areas of deficiency. This is the "you bring this, I'll bring that" approach.

The data is clear: if your employees are motivated and encouraged to use their talents, it is far more likely that your bottom line is happy.

Or, for our purposes, you can take the opportunity to help this prized member of your team discover their Blue Flame. In doing so, you can often help them redirect their talents, passions, and purpose into a more appropriate role—whether inside your company or beyond—where they can have greater impact.

I gave Sandra a heads-up that I wanted to use our regular weekly one-on-one time to discuss the evolving leadership needs in customer service.

As she walked into my office for our next meeting, her shoulders a bit slumped and her head hung low, I got the sense she thought I was going to fire her.

I hopped up to the whiteboard and drew three intersecting lines representing the Blue Flame.

"Sandra, you are an exceedingly talented woman. And as we both know, the types of talents you have are different from the types of talents that are going to be needed in this next chapter of our evolution in customer service." She gasped a bit as I acknowledged the elephant in the room, and her body language seemed to suggest that her pink slip would follow.

"So, I want to talk not about customer service, but about *you*, and figure out how we can use your talents in the ways that will have the highest impact on the business. I know how much you care about this company and know that you care about being successful, so I imagine that you're similarly interested in this conversation."

She reluctantly leaned in, her guard clearly dropping a smidge. She still wasn't sure where this was going. After all, under the company's prior ownership, if you weren't cutting the mustard in your role, you simply found a pink slip and a cardboard box on your desk. This created a general sense of fear and insecurity among staff.

"Let me tell you about a core belief I have, Sandra: amazing things happen when we can get people like you playing at the intersection point of three powerful forces: *what they can do best, what they find invigorating, and what they care deeply about*. Or in short form, their talents, their passions, and their purpose."

I pointed to the intersection of the three lines I had drawn. "When these forces collide, a powerful chemical reaction can be ignited. I call it the *Blue Flame*. Can you picture a magnificent, powerful Blue Flame? I would try to draw it, but you know how atrocious my whiteboard art is!" She laughed.

"See, when we can get every person in this business playing in the vicinity of their Blue Flame," pointing enthusiastically at the intersection of the three lines, "that's the recipe for a business that catches fire and becomes wildly successful."

"Like the '92 dream team!" she piped in, showing her colors as a vintage NBA fan and clearly getting engaged in the conversation now. "You know—when everyone is brilliant in their own particular way and playing their own role exceptionally well, but it all comes together as a great team performance?"

"Exactly. So, we need to think about this conversation in a different way than you might be accustomed to. Let's set aside the role that you are playing right now. We can come back to that later. Instead, let's re-center on *your* brilliance, and unpack where your greatest talents, your passions, and your purpose lie," I said as I pointed to the three lines on the whiteboard.

I moved my finger over to the *Talents* axis, and I asked Sandra to tell me about what she felt she was best at. What comes easily to her. What other people who she worked with, when asked, would say that Sandra can do better than anyone else on the team.

We began to build up a makeshift "strengths inventory." You could see Sandra's confidence start to crescendo as she began to see her talents written on the board in front of her. I sensed that she had lost sight of these.

We shifted gears and began exploring her *Passions* axis—the activities that she finds to be invigorating. *What were the things that gave her a great buzz when she was doing them? The types of job activities that she found herself getting deeply immersed and almost lost in?*

It turns out she really loved planning things. Getting people coordinated, and working through a task list was invigorating to her. She drew a lot of energy from keeping things moving, and getting things done.

And as she shifted over to the *Purpose* axis, it quickly emerged that what Sandra cared deeply about, what brought her meaning, was taking care of people—like her team—and making sure that everyone had what they needed.

In that light, it made complete sense that she loved to throw dinner parties. And the meticulousness—a signature talent—that I saw in a work environment applied in the context of hosting a dinner party as well. Everything at Sandra's dinner party had to be just right. It wouldn't be just a successful dinner party; it would be the *perfect* dinner party, because her guests deserved it. Every detail was carefully thought through, from matching the linens to her guests' favorite colors, to ensuring a menu that appealed to different tastes. And she pulled it off every time (except, she pointed out, for that one time the dog jumped onto the counter and ate the honey baked ham).

With an increasingly clear shared view of what Sandra could do best, what invigorated her, and what she cared about, we started to unpack together where her Blue Flame could be applied to have the greatest impact in her professional life.

We quickly agreed that in light of what we had uncovered, she was not the best fit to lead the change that was needed in the company's customer service organization. It didn't mean that she was a failure or untalented. It simply meant that her talents, passions, and purpose didn't align with the unique needs of that role. The job simply wasn't a good fit, and we agreed that it didn't make a lot of sense to keep trying to "fit a square peg into a round hole" if we could apply Sandra's Blue Flame in an area that could have considerably more impact.

"Let me run an idea past you," I said as I thought out loud. "We happen to need someone to oversee sales support. This is a really crucial role for us right now. All of our growth plans rely on the sales team operating as a well-equipped, well-oiled machine, and the sales team needs support to do this. They need someone who is going to make sure they have everything they need to be successful: training, sales kit, software tools, and logistics support. You name it. And we need someone who is very methodical, because these things need thorough follow-up, they need attention to detail. Our sales folks can't show up to a big presentation without the materials they need."

She cracked a smile. I continued, "There are also some big events to plan and organize—like the annual sales conference. That is a big investment and it absolutely has to work. We need someone who is highly skilled at organizing events, who has the types of talents that you do in planning, coordination, and execution. You could think of it almost like a big dinner party."

I smiled at her now. "Do you know anyone who might fit that bill?"

She smiled back even bigger.

We left the meeting each aglow from the breakthrough that this conversation created. As we walked out of the room, Sandra turned to me and said: "No boss of mine has ever had this kind of conversation with me. *This could change everything!*"

The following week, we moved Sandra into the new sales support leadership role, and she went on to crush it. I checked in a few weeks later and she was absolutely beaming.

"This is going to be great," she told me. "I was very nervous at first, but *this* is me. I can be great at this. I want to thank you for giving me the opportunity. Customer service was always my thing and I didn't really see myself in sales. But it took coming back to what I do best, and what gives me the most energy to better understand where I can have the most impact. And I've gotta tell you, I'm loving it! I can really make a difference here."

Sandra's story is just one case study in the performance-unlocking potential of Blue Flame conversations. But this practice—and a culture that promotes this type of exploration—isn't commonplace in many businesses.

As leaders, we need to take more time to have meaningful Blue Flame conversations with those in our charge. Given that *people* are the fundamental building blocks of businesses in the knowledge economy, ultimately, our success as leaders depends on it.

But what gets in the way of focusing our time and attention here? I have a theory.

Observation #3: Leaders fail to make time to discuss Blue Flames because they get caught up in the more urgent demands of their job.
Many of us are addicted to urgency: the fires that need putting out and the emails that need prompt responses. There's a thrill and satisfaction in cranking through the punch-list of tasks that give us that gratifying little shot of dopamine every time we cross one off. We strive to knock down as many pins as quickly as we can.

if you care about your employees and the success of your company, you will make time to invest in setting their Blue Flame ablaze.

Researchers who led a 2018 study published in the *Journal of Consumer Research* concluded that "people may choose to perform urgent tasks with short completion windows, instead of important tasks with larger outcomes, because important tasks are more difficult and further away from goal completion, urgent tasks involve more immediate and certain payoffs, or people want to finish the urgent tasks first and then work on important tasks later."[8]

---

[8] Meng Zhu, Yang Yang, and Christopher K Hsee, "Mere Urgency Effect," *Journal of Consumer Research*, Volume 45, Issue 3, October 2018, Pages 673–690, https://academic.oup.com/jcr/advance-article-abstract/doi/10.1093/jcr/ucy008/4847790?redirectedFrom=fulltext.

In his book *First Things First,* famed author Stephen Covey contends that this addiction to crossing things off a list gets in the way of the real stuff of leadership. We can't thrive as leaders by focusing strictly on the things that are right in front of us. We need to identify things that will have a long-lasting, positive impact, and then prioritize them. It's time that we "schedule our priorities" instead of just "prioritizing our schedule."

For many people, their "First Things First" are personal relationships with family and friends. For many leaders, the "First Things First" should be pouring energy into your people and helping them to soar ... undoubtedly one of *the* most important things a leader will do over the long term.

President Dwight Eisenhower, our 34th president, offers us a productivity strategy to combat something that author Charles Hummel called the "tyranny of the urgent." Eisenhower's technique, known nowadays as the "Eisenhower Boxes," asks us to score each thing competing for our time or attention on two axes—its *importance* (high/low) and its *urgency*. Then, use that understanding to make decisions about how to use your limited time.

What many leaders realize when they do this exercise is that the urgent stuff is running their lives and taking time away from the things that they know can have the largest impact in the long term.

The truth is, if you care about your employees and the success of your company, you will make time to invest in setting their Blue Flame ablaze.

Observation #4: It is easy to get too wrapped up in ourselves.

We have our own bills to pay, our own career to grow, our own stakeholders to manage, and our own Blue Flame to find. Sure, we would love to help those around us to grow and thrive, but we've got to take care of number one before we can support others. We've got our own mounting pile of things to deal with.

The book *The Outward Mindset* draws the distinction between two types of mentalities: an *inward* mindset in which we behave in ways that are calculated to benefit ourselves, and an *outward* mindset in which we focus on others, and on the collective.

Leaders who function from an inward mindset—whether consciously or not—can sabotage their own success. They get in their own way.

They strive to be successful in their self-serving missions, but by doing so from an inward mindset, they alienate and neglect the people on their teams whom they are depending on to help them be successful. Leaders functioning from an inward mindset can quickly fall back on a command-and-control, dictatorial way of leading. Without this iron-fisted type of leadership and the fear it can create, they worry no one would want to follow them. So they end up tricking themselves into thinking that leadership comes through control.

Leaders who get wrapped up in themselves in this way can cause all sorts of long-term collateral damage. You don't have to look too far in the business news to find recent high-profile examples of the cost of an inward mindset.

The Outward Mindset offers that "a [leader] with an outward mindset will hold him/herself accountable to accomplish his/her own objectives in a way that makes it *easier*, not harder, for his colleagues to succeed in their responsibilities. When my mindset is outward, I am alive to and interested in other people and their needs. I see others as people who I am open to helping."[9]

In short, focusing on what *our people* need, is often the ticket to helping us achieve what *we need*.

---

[9] Arbinger Institute. *The Outward Mindset: Seeing Beyond Ourselves.* Berrett-Koehler Publishers, 2016.

Observation #5: Many of us haven't been taught how to have these conversations.
"Sure, I'd love to have Blue Flame conversations, but these kinds of conversations can be tough. How do I get someone to open up about what they are great at? About what they love? How do I help them make sense of it all?"

For many leaders, the discomfort stems from a common issue: many small and mid-sized companies don't invest in equipping their leaders with the skills and confidence to have these sorts of conversations.

I have seen this often. In small companies—and even large ones—great employees are promoted to manager for being good at their job, or because they are the "next man/woman up," irrespective of whether their own Blue Flame lends itself to the managerial role they are being thrust into. But they are given the promotion anyways, shown to their new fancy desk and given their badge, and told: "Good luck out there ... you'll figure it out."

Some figure it out. But this leadership stuff can be tough! And one of the most common struggles new leaders encounter is in having crucial exchanges with their employees, like Blue Flame conversations.

Rest assured: this book was written in a way that will equip you with the mindset, tools, questions, and language to have powerful Blue Flame discussions with your team.

Observation #6: Some of us avoid these conversations because we're worried our people might leave us.
What if you help someone find their Blue Flame, only to realize they are suddenly no longer a fit for your company?

Entertainer Steve Harvey, famous for his annual flubs as host of the Miss Universe pageant, weighed in during an interview with *Fortune* magazine: "If your talent isn't useful to the company you work for, that's a sure sign that you're going to feel not happy about waking up going into work, a sure sign that you're going to feel like your life is in a rut, and a sure sign that you're going to feel like there's got to be more to life than this right here."

As a manager, sure, there is the real practical reality of needing to retain good people. But here's the flaw in this way of thinking: if an employee isn't operating at full power in your organization, it is not good for anyone. So don't waste everyone's time and money!

Leaders need to be willing to sacrifice what they believe is in the good of the company—keeping good employees—for what is actually good for the company—helping employees find their Blue Flame, even if that means them leaving the company. The reality is, what's best for the employee is best for the company, and vice versa.

IN CASE YOU MISSED IT: THE KEY IDEAS

The Case for Putting People First: Too often, companies fail to prioritize lighting their people up, and they leave a lot on the table as a result. As we have discussed, there is a tight correlation between the degree to which companies invest in bringing the best out of their people and real hard-dollar results.

Urgent vs. Important: Too often, leaders fail to make time to discuss Blue Flames because they get caught up in the more urgent demands of their job. But there is a difference between what is important and what is urgent. Successful leaders make time to invest in these conversations with their people, recognizing that their long-term success depends on getting the best that their people have to give.

Focusing Outward: We can sabotage our success as leaders when we get caught up in ourselves, even when it is unintentional. The antidote? Look outward. Focusing on what *our people* need is ultimately the ticket to getting the sense of gratification, worth, and success that we need as leaders. And our people need to feel lit up by the work they are doing in order to bring their best stuff.

Teaching to Fish: Too many small and mid-sized companies fail to teach their managers how to have crucial conversations. Equipping leaders with the tools to have Blue Flame conversations is a key that can unlock new levels of performance in a company.

PART

Talents: Do What You Do Best

CHAPTER 4

What Can You Do Best?

At the beginning of the twenty-first century, psychologist Martin Seligman helped pioneer a new movement in the field of psychology, one that laid the tracks for the Blue Flame. To understand the importance of this new ideology, let's rewind a bit:

A witty, well-educated New York native, Seligman began his psychology career studying learned helplessness in dogs—something that my lazy and emotionally needy rescue pup can surely identify with. Seligman began to reflect on how twentieth-century psychology seemed focused entirely on unwellness: on mental illness rather than well-being, on fixing what was broken.

In its early years, psychology had adopted the disease model of its more grown-up sister profession, medicine, and focused on investigating and classifying what is wrong with people in order to find ways to make them better. In essence, the goal was to help to make miserable people less miserable.

To give well-deserved credit, this disease model had a massive positive impact on mentally unwell populations. Of the sixteen most common classifications of disorders—such as depression and alcoholism—fourteen are now treatable, and two are curable.

The focus on diseased and debilitated people, however, overlooked a huge population of humans—the relatively untroubled ones—whom Seligman thought could greatly benefit from the field's growing understanding of the human mind and behavior. Why, Seligman wondered, wasn't psychology focused on helping these people to thrive, rather than just survive? Couldn't this same understanding of human psychology that was used to help the unwell get better also be used to find interventions that could lead to happier, more fulfilling lives for the rest of us?

Seligman wrote, "Psychology should be able to help document what kinds of families result in children who *flourish*, what work settings support the greatest satisfaction among workers, what policies result in the strongest civil engagement, and how people's lives can be most worth living." This came from the January 2000 issue of *American Psychologist*—an issue that was devoted entirely to contributions from leading thinkers in this new field that went on to become known as *positive psychology*.[10]

Seligman posited that psychology should be just as concerned with human strength as it should be with weakness. His own epiphany, as he tells it, came from an everyday conversation with his five-year old daughter, Nikki.

He was doing some weeding in his garden and confesses that he became irritated by young Nikki's shenanigans as he was hard at work. She was dancing around, throwing weeds up in the air, and singing as her father toiled away. In a moment of reactivity, he had enough and hissed at his playful young daughter, as many of us would find ourselves doing in this situation.

Nikki walked off, chastened. A short time later, she came back to respond to her irritated and dismissive father.

"Daddy," said Nikki, "do you remember the time before my fifth birthday? From the time I was three to the time I was five, I was a whiner. I whined every day. When I turned five, I decided not to whine anymore. That was the hardest thing I've ever done. And if I can stop whining, you can stop being such a grouch."

Ouch. Well played, Nikki. Her insightful, yet crushing comment had the impact of a precision-guided Hellfire missile. Seligman says he had three waves of insight as a result of the devastating strike.

First, he realized that Nikki had stopped whining all by herself without any help from grumpy old dad. He recognized that kids can improve and grow without intervention from their parents. How cool.

Second, Seligman admitted that he was, indeed, a grouch—"a nimbus cloud in a house full of sunshine"—and that any achievements of his had been in spite of his grumpiness, not because of it.

---

[10] Martin E. P. Seligman and Mihaly Csikszentmihalyi, "Positive Psychology: An Introduction," *American Psychologist*, January 2000, https://ppc.sas.upenn.edu/sites/default/files/ppintroarticle.pdf.

Finally, raising Nikki should be about recognizing her wonderful strengths, nurturing and amplifying those strengths, and helping her find ways to use those strengths. Throughout the afternoon in the garden, Nikki showed such a playful and imaginative creativity. When looking at the situation through this lens, a less reactive response came to mind: *How could I encourage and use her talents to get the gardening done in a way that helps me, and is still engaging for her?*

Beyond improving his relationship with his daughter, Seligman's epiphany inspired him to set out to change the study of psychology.

He began with two simple questions, the seeds that would sprout into the game-changing field of positive psychology:

How can the decades-long focus on fixing patients be complemented with a new focus on actively enhancing their lives?

And what if every person was encouraged to nurture his or her strengths, rather than scolded into fixing their shortcomings?

STUCK IN FIX-IT MODE

In the same way that it was instinctively easy for Seligman to see what was *wrong* with his daughter's behavior in that moment, we humans have a funny way of fixating on our own deficiencies, and ruminating on our mistakes.

As Marcus Buckingham—an ex-Gallup leader who pioneered the organization's work on employee engagement that we covered in Chapter 2—said, "Most people are more fascinated by who they *aren't* and how to fix it, instead of who they *are* and how to leverage it."

Fixating on your weaknesses may feel like a familiar concept.

Picture this everyday scenario: You say something inarticulately in a meeting, one of those "foot in mouth" comments. No sooner are the words out of your mouth than you are mentally beating up on yourself. "What was I thinking? What will they think of me? What shade and size is the pink slip that will be waiting on my desk?"

I still remember one of those instances from an early part of my career. During a debrief discussion after an important investment meeting with the partners of our firm, they asked what I thought about the investment opportunity. This was it. My chance to shine.

But I'm one of those "I need time to gather my thoughts first" types. I tried as best I could to disguise my unpreparedness and ignorance with a stuttering parade of fancy words like "barriers to entry" and "operating leverage," but they quickly saw through the nonsensical jargon, which was a thinly veiled attempt to convince them that I actually knew what I was talking about.

I still remember the look on their faces, which screamed, "What in tarnation is this young pipsqueak even talking about?" I ruminated on this and ragged on myself for several weeks afterward. I still cringe thinking about it. Oy vey.

Stack a few of these up over time and it can start to feel like we have our own personalized blooper reel playing on repeat in our heads. This self-esteem shattering montage features our most earth-shaking face-plants, our most monumental meltdowns, and our most epic blunders.

The impulse to ruminate on our mistakes or weaknesses in this way stems from a thing known as "negativity bias," and unfortunately, our brains are hardwired for it.

Innovations in MRI have transformed our understanding of how our brains work by allowing us to see which areas of the brain "light up" when research subjects are going through various experiences. It allows us to actually watch negativity bias happening in our brains as it occurs.

Most people are more fascinated by who they aren't and how to fix it, instead of who they are and how to leverage it.

In one experiment, subjects were shown a collection of positive, neutral, or negative images while researchers monitored their brain activity with an MRI scanner. The scans showed that the negative images were generating a far stronger response in the cerebral cortex—the brain's information processing center—than either positive or neutral images. The higher level of neural activity in the cerebral cortex produced by negative images shows that our brains are especially interested in these. In effect, our brains are saying, "Take note! This negative stuff matters!"

That's why our blooper reel keeps playing on repeat in our heads. Our brains retain the unsavory stuff very well. They can't get enough of it.

There is a sound evolutionary explanation for this. For long periods of human evolution, in hostile environments it was critical to our survival to be especially alert to negative things in life that posed a risk. This behavior regularly meant the difference between life or death.

We tend to closely examine the deficiencies and failures, and overlook the bright spots.

In the Paleolithic era, you may have been enjoying a barbecued woolly mammoth steak and a warm glass of primitive booze made from chewed root, sitting around a roaring fire with your fellow hunters and gatherers—cavemen and cavewomen and cavebabies. But you were also on high alert—one eye on the next savory bite, and the other scanning the environment around you for bad stuff.

That rustle you heard in the undergrowth behind you just might be a saber-toothed tiger, and your brain needed you to pay attention. When the racket in the bushes was, in fact, a ferocious predator, and it pounced, you were ready to rumble. Your brain had you at the ready to chase off the predator with a blunt Smilodon tusk, or unleash your pet hyena on the encroaching predator to scare it off.

Whew! That was a close one.

You survived the semi-regular tiger ordeal, and because of the bravery you exhibited, you became so irresistible to your gawking tribemates of the opposite sex that you were able to procreate. And, voila, these "pay attention to the bad stuff" genes that kept you alive were passed down to the next generation. And the next. And so on.

But remember your popular caveman buddy, Mr. Happy-Go-Lucky? The one with the rosy cheeks and the perpetually sunny outlook? He didn't fare so well.

When he heard the same commotion in the undergrowth, Happy thought: *Nah. Just some kids messing around.* Then he went back to playing gleefully with a stick. Next thing he knew, he was caught in the maw of the massive beast. CHOMP.

As a direct result of young Happy-Go-Lucky's early demise, his carefree, glass-half-full, "nothing bad ever happens to me" genes got wiped from the evolutionary gene pool.

In this day and age, saber-toothed tigers and similar threats aren't as prominent in most parts of the world. But these outdated genes and adaptive responses are still in us, as relics of prior eras of human development. Unfortunately, they don't serve us as well nowadays as they once did.

It is, in part, a perfectly natural biological response for humans like you and me to focus on the bad stuff. We feel the pain of loss or insult more strongly than we feel the pleasure of gain or praise.

So it might feel natural to obsess over what's wrong with people, including ourselves, rather than focusing on what's right with them. It's because we are looking for hidden threats our brains want us to learn from.

Imagine that you are my parents—don't worry, it's just a thought experiment. One day, Little Dan Cremons brings his report card home from school. Drumroll, please.

Reading	A
Math	F
Social Studies	A
Science	B+

What's your most likely reaction?

Is it "Dan! Three As and a B? That's amazing! You're so smart, little fella. Let's go get that new guitar you wanted!"

Or is it *"Daniel!* How many times have we told you to pay more attention to your math classes? Do you want to go to college or not? You're grounded until we see some improvement here!"

Negativity bias says that it is perfectly instinctive—though not entirely productive, as we'll soon discuss—that we home in on the pitiful math score, and tune out the commendable performance in reading, social studies, and English.

We tend to closely examine the deficiencies and failures, and overlook the bright spots. This same phenomenon shows up in the workplace.

Picture the following everyday example: You and your team are looking at a metrics dashboard containing some of the key performance indicators that you use to run your business. Those KPIs are coded by red-yellow-green based on the degree to which they're on track. Green means good, and red means something is off track.

As you scan down the dashboard in your weekly meeting, what jumps off the page? For most of us, it is the reds. We quickly home in on the issue areas. Oftentimes, this can be a useful inclination in a managerial context—as it can be a better use of management's time to focus on helping things that are off track to get back on the rails.

This same negativity bias gives us a much sharper recollection of the "areas for development" from our prior performance reviews, than it does the glowing praise we received from our boss. Cognitively, the negative emotions associated with the critical feedback are processed more thoroughly and retained more prominently than the positive praise.

The problem with this, of course, is that when we spend too much time focused on what we don't do well, we lose sight of where our unique brilliance lies. Our inclination to "find and fix" can cause us to fail to notice what's of fundamental importance in life and leadership: What's *right*. What's *working*. What is *brilliant*—or can be made so, as Seligman dreamed.

Some of us haven't discovered our unique brilliance altogether. As the Buddha said, "Everyone is gifted here, but some of us never opened their package."

As a result, we don't figure out how to use our brilliance to maximize our impact on our companies, our communities, and the world. Sometimes, we don't even believe we have something to offer.

What a tragedy. The world needs every ounce of our brilliance. It needs us to shine brightly.

DO WHAT YOU DO BEST

The founders of the Life is Good Company, known for their colorful T-shirts with whimsical little stick figures that spout profound life wisdom, once shared, "This is really what our whole brand, idea, and philosophy is based on: We all have limited resources, and when we wake up in the morning, we can decide to focus on what's wrong with us, or we can focus on what's right."

In that same vein, Martin Seligman has simple but powerful advice for us: "The recipe for the 'good life' is knowing what your greatest talents are, and then recrafting your life—your work, your love, your play, your friendship, your parenting—to use them as much as you possibly can."

This advice starts to seem even more sensible when we recognize that we as human beings face some real, practical constraints in life. Among them, the most finite and nonrenewable resource we have is our time.

In his book *Outliers*, Malcolm Gladwell popularized the idea that it takes 10,000 hours of one's time to truly master any particular skill, whether it's playing the violin, figure-skating, or quantum physics.

This is known as "The 10-Year Rule," since that's roughly how much time, Gladwell observed, a dedicated person needs to become a master at something. In every one of life's endeavors, achieving excellence requires a lot of time.

But there are only so many hours in the day, and days in the year. And if you spend your time trying to be a little bit good at everything, it statistically reduces your chances of being great at anything. This is a key concept for leaders to grasp.

It is for this reason that the book *First, Break All the Rules,* co-authored by Marcus Buckingham and Curt Coffman and based on one of the largest-scale studies of managerial effectiveness ever conducted, advises us: "Don't waste time trying to put in what was left out. Try to draw out what is already in there. That is hard enough."[11]

When we have our eyes open for it, we can see the challenges with "trying to put in what was left out," and the benefits of "drawing out—*and using*—what is already in there" in everyday ways.

As I am writing this chapter, the NFL Pro Bowl Skills Showdown is playing in

---

[11] Marcus Buckingham and Curt Coffman, *First, Break All the Rules* (Simon & Schuster, 2005)

the background. Players who are chosen for the Pro Bowl compete in fun skills challenges like precision passing competitions, obstacle racing, and dodgeball.

Among the competitors is Jarvis Landry, a wide receiver for the Cleveland Browns who is quick as an antelope and has hands as sticky as a tree frog's. Landry has just come off a pitiful performance representing the NFC in the passing challenge—a perfectly understandable outcome for a wide receiver competing in a quarterback's competition.

But several minutes into the second round of NFC vs. AFC dodgeball, Landry finds himself on the losing end of a four-men-on-two situation in a must-win game. The stakes are high, and bragging rights are on the line.

In case you live under a rock and haven't seen the 2004 film *Dodgeball*, the truest underdog story in the sports film genre, there are essentially two skills that matter in dodgeball: throwing the ball in an attempt to strike your competitors, and evading or catching balls thrown at you. In dodgeball, getting opposing players out most often happens by hitting them with a thrown ball, but you can also get someone out by catching a ball.

Back to the action: there Landry and his teammate are, with two dodgeballs in hand and four competitors staring them down from across the centerline, like a couple of water buffalo surrounded by a ravenous pack of lions.

In an unusual strategic move, Landry rolls his two balls over to the other team—which is like giving an opposing army your last two missiles. This leaves him virtually defenseless since you can block an opponent's throw using a ball in your own hands to bounce the attacking ball away.

But Landry has a plan. You see, he gets paid $15 million per year to *catch* balls thrown at him, not to *throw* balls He is a receiver, not a quarterback. So he gives the opposition more balls to throw at him and waits for the attack. Now he's left with only two options: to dodge the opponents' balls or make a clean catch, which would knock his opponent out of the game.

Two of the contenders take aim at Landry and fire their soft foam ammunition almost simultaneously, right on target. Landry catches the first ball, discards it, and a split second later catches the second incoming. Two opponents out! The contest is down to two-on-two.

But just as momentum is building, Landry's teammate's ball gets caught by a sure-handed opponent. He's out. Two-on-one!

Landry is the last man standing on his side. He uses his own ball, clutched tightly in both hands, to block a perfectly aimed throw heading straight for his midriff. On the attack, one of his two opponents makes a colossal error, foot-faulting on the centerline and suffering instant and embarrassing disqualification. It is now one-on-one!

Landry, a ball in each hand, squares off with his remaining opponent. A perfect throw comes straight at him, with the speed and precision of a sniper shot. Landry speedily discards his own balls with a flick of his hands and catches the incoming missile. It's all over. Landry prevails!

Apart from reminding us how much fun a good ol' fashioned game of dodgeball is, this example also illustrates a key principle of the Blue Flame in action. As evidenced by his pitiful performance in the passing challenge, Jarvis Landry isn't a good thrower—and he doesn't really try to be. But he *is* a great catcher, and he knows to lean on his talent heavily, especially when the stakes are high.

HOW TO THINK ABOUT TALENTS

Each of us is profoundly unique, and not just in a feel-good, motherhood-and-apple-pie kind of way. (Cue the cheek-pinching from Grandma—"You're such a unique and special kid!")

Think about it. You are the first person ever to be born with your unique genetic makeup. This individuality makes each of us one of a kind—genetically, psychologically, and cognitively—given that the makeup of each of our brains is completely unique.

Research has shown that even identical twins don't actually have identically *expressed* genes, despite starting life with a matching genetic blueprint.

This unique brain wiring equips each of us with our own unique set of talents.

But what does *talent* mean? The term can become misconstrued, as it often gets mixed up in a buzzword stew with other similar terms like "strengths," "skills," and "unique abilities." At their core, these ideas all refer to roughly the same general concept: things we're good at and areas where we can perform effectively.

But to really understand and appreciate the power of talents, it is important to drill down into the nuance.

When we talk about talents, do we mean a talent for skateboarding, or business finance, or for telling jokes? Or are talents things like empathy and compassion? Or technical things like knowing how to write code or perform open-heart surgery?

The book I referenced earlier, *First, Break All the Rules,* offers one of the more useful constructs for understanding talents.

The book distinguishes between *knowledge, skills,* and *talent*, three interrelated but distinct ideas that often get conflated. Let's break it down.

Knowledge refers to *things that you know*, and comes in two flavors: factual and experiential.

Factual knowledge is the information we have acquired as we go through life. For instance, I know that the square of the hypotenuse of a right-angle triangle is equal to the sum of the other two sides squared. I also know that a discounted cash flow analysis will give me a useful measure of the value of a company, and that Steely Dan is the best rock band in history. These are pieces of factual knowledge, things we have come to know and understand because we learned them clearly and explicitly. Okay, fine, the Steely Dan example might be subjective.

Our talents strengthen and grow more powerful if they are put to good and constant use.

Experiential knowledge, on the other hand, is the knowledge we acquire about certain patterns and connections between things. Your experience of playing tennis tells you that a ball served in a certain way is likely to bounce up at a particular speed, height, and direction, or your experience of working with people across different business functions tells you that a particular person will likely be most effective in a certain role.

By contrast, **skills** are *proficiencies that can be learned.* You can learn how to play the euphonium, how to serve a tennis ball at over a hundred miles an hour, or how to do double-entry bookkeeping. We can learn new *skills* until late in life, provided we stay in good shape mentally and physically, and our underlying *talents* lend themselves to the development of these skills.

Talents are neither skills nor knowledge, but they lay the foundation for both.

First, Break All the Rules defines a talent as "*a recurring pattern of thought, feeling, or behavior.*" That is, an ability or way of thinking that tends to show up for you time and time again, in different contexts and situations. You're most likely already thinking of the talents you know you have at this moment. And no, being able to sing every word of "Bohemian Rhapsody" in near perfect pitch is not a talent, that's a skill.

> **When we are faced with a challenge that plays to our talents and stretches us to the limits of what we can achieve—but is not impossible—we can experience "flow."**

Here's an example. A talent of mine is *envisioning*: picturing what could be there when nothing is. I am able to apply this talent constructively in all sorts of ways, including in helping leadership teams to imagine what their vision for the future could look like. Or imagining how I want my new deck to look when there's nothing but a patch of dead grass there today.

Envisioning isn't a new pattern for me, it has been with me for a while. It's this same talent that I put to work for hours on end during my childhood, sketching elaborate houses or cities on graph paper. It's the same talent that consumed endless hours of my teenage and college years as I wrote and improvised music with other musicians.

Envisioning has been my trusted wingman for as long as I can remember. And, using it over time and in different stages of life, I've only sharpened it and learned to use it more skillfully. This regular pattern of envisioning has strengthened the neural pathways in my brain that are responsible for this talent. At this point, I probably couldn't shake it if I tried.

As is the case with many of our predispositions—or talents—they can often come off as abnormal or counterproductive to people who don't see their value, or when used in the wrong context. My wife, for instance, frequently has to nudge me back into consciousness when I get lost in an imaginative daydream when we're out to dinner. She's threatened to make me wear a canine shock collar to zap me back to attention, but luckily for me, she is a bit self-conscious about the fact that this might be frowned upon in a public setting.

There is surely some amount of innate brain wiring that is responsible for this talent. And some of this talent probably arose from adaptation early in my life. Some nature, and some nurture.

However much of this talent is attributable to *nature* (biological predispositions), and however much is attributable to *nurture* (the influence of one's environment), most of our talents tend to take root early in life and lay the foundation for much of our skill and knowledge attainment over time. If we have the seeds of the *precision* talent in us early in life, chances are, we will become good at (and enjoy) the skill of *algebra* when we get into school. We may naturally gravitate toward being an accountant when we get older.

Over time, our talents strengthen and grow more powerful if they are put to good and constant use.

This idea of "nature vs. nurture" as it relates to talent formation is a complex area, but when you boil down the research, think of it like this: we are all born with the seedlings of unique talents (this is the "nature" part, based on the unique ingredients baked into our DNA). These seedlings may get watered, or in other cases dried out, based on a host of "nurture" factors, like our environment, upbringing, access to resources, effort, hard work, and deep practice.

Some people's seedlings—if watered by training, exposure, and the environment they develop within—sprout into a very visible, prominent talent. Talents like intuition, or creativity, or empathy, or persistence. And like muscles, the more we use these talents, the stronger they become.

In this way, talent development becomes self-reinforcing.

Let's say some combination of your nature and your nurture conspired to create in you a budding talent for language and abstraction. And let's say you learn that this talent can be applied to writing poetry. So, you give poetry a whirl and it feels good to do something that plays nicely with how your brain seems to be wired. You start to enjoy writing poetry and you do it more and more often. And as you do it more often, your talent for language and abstraction and your skill for writing poetry strengthen. And so the pattern continues.

It is in this way that a powerful *virtuous cycle* tends to form when we understand and lean into our talents.

TALENTS IN ACTION

"The person born with a talent they are meant to use will find their greatest happiness and success in using it." —*Johann Wolfgang von Goethe*

Lori Goler, Facebook's head of human resources, had been following the work of Buckingham and Coffman (the guys who wrote *First, Break all the Rules* and were pioneers of the strengths movement) as she built and led successful teams for juggernauts like eBay and Disney.

She instituted their core idea—*focusing on strengths, not fixing weaknesses*—as a centerpiece of Facebook's wildly successful engagement-focused culture. She notes that, "While intuitively it seems 'nice' to match people's strengths to their roles in order to maximize engagement, the success of the practice goes much deeper than that."

To understand how this idea has created such a vibrant and high-performance environment at Facebook, we must dip our toe into the research completed in the 1970s at the University of Chicago by Hungarian psychologist Mihaly Csikszentmihalyi. His groundbreaking idea, known simply as "flow," centers around an "optimal state of consciousness where we feel—and perform—our best." Csikszentmihalyi suggested that we experience flow when we are experiencing conditions of "optimal challenge."

When things are too easy, we quickly become bored. When things are way beyond us, we feel anxious and dejected. But, when we are faced with a challenge that plays to our talents and stretches us to the limits of what we can achieve—but is not impossible—we can experience "flow."

Flow is so powerful that in a ten-year study conducted by McKinsey, top executives reported being five times more productive when in flow.[12] When we are experiencing flow, we are able to concentrate intensely for long periods of time, and often fail to notice how long we have been absorbed in our task. We feel we are working "at the height of our powers," with relevant information coming readily to mind and solutions to complex problems presenting themselves clearly.

---

[12] Mike Hoefflinger, "How Facebook Keeps Its Employees the Happiest, According to a Former Insider," *Business Insider*, April 11, 2017, https://www.businessinsider.com/how-facebook-keeps-employees-happy-2017-4.

On a collective level, when a group of people each find their flow states, they can achieve a thing called social flow. If you set foot in a Facebook office, you can feel this flow immediately. The place feels alive, a community of committed, mission-aligned people who—independently and as a collective—seem totally dialed-in. They appear to be vibrating on the same wavelength, like a world-class jazz ensemble immersed in improvisation, who seem to be operating from a shared group consciousness.

Insiders and outsiders alike attribute Facebook's meteoric success, in part, to the emphasis on creating a potent culture focused on tapping into the native genius of its people, and the sense of flow that doing so can create.

Based on data collected by Payscale from 33,500 tech workers, Facebook employees were the most satisfied (96 percent) and the least stressed (44 percent) of the top eighteen technology companies in the study. Facebook was number two overall (and number one in Technology), in Glassdoor's "Best Places to Work in 2017." They maintained a rating of 4.5 out of 5 stars, with 92 percent of employees likely to recommend the company to a friend, and 92 percent of their employees had a positive outlook for the company's future.[13]

In a knowledge business like Facebook, the ability to retain great talent—in an age where there is cutthroat competition for the best technical talent—is *everything*. As Goler says, "The thing that separates people who stay for a long time [from those] who make the choice to leave is how they score themselves [in internal self-assessments and employee surveys] on whether they're playing to their strengths."

But all this talk of using talents in the workplace necessitates that we have a clear-minded, high-fidelity view of what our talents are, and what they aren't.

Remember Martin Seligman? The guy whose daughter Nikki told him to stop being such a jerk? When Martin Seligman took that moment to heart, he was embarking on a quest to use the study and practice of psychology to help people lead richer and more fulfilling lives, instead of strictly focusing on people with problems that are in need of fixing. His research led him to the groundbreaking—but still rather commonsensical—conclusion that people will be happier and more fulfilled when they are doing what they can do best.

---

[13] Ibid.

Working with fellow psychologist Christopher Peterson, Seligman created what is now known as the Values in Action Inventory of Strengths (VIA-IS), which set out to classify character strengths: things like Creativity, Love of Learning, Perseverance, Kindness, Social Intelligence, Teamwork, and Humility. They identified twenty-four strengths in all.

Using their strengths inventory, Seligman and his colleagues set out to see what happened when people identified their core strengths and began making better use of them in their daily lives and at work.

Compared to the control group, participants who used their strengths in this way *for just one week* reported increased levels of happiness that *persisted for six months*.[14]

Other studies showed that when people were encouraged to make greater use of their core strengths at work, they developed a greater passion for their work, and this in turn led to a greater sense of well-being *and* better work performance.

Elsewhere, Donald Clifton, Curt Coffman, and Marcus Buckingham conducted a survey of 80,000 managers in 2,500 different business units of various kinds. Their goal was to further understand the effect of strengths-use at work.

The survey's findings proved the basic principle of the "strengths" movement, one that leaders like you and me need to take note of: the most objectively successful managers weren't fixated on trying to correct people's weaknesses; they instead focused on playing to people's strengths. When they did this, they maximized the contributions of their employees, and made them happier and more fulfilled in their work.

The research led to a very important insight: that "casting is everything." It turns out that the best way to turn talent into performance is to put people in roles where they are doing what their talents have them hardwired to do best.

What's more, studies have even drawn a connection between greater use of strengths and greater income.

★ ★ ★

---

[14] Christopher Peterson and Martin E. P. Seligman, *Character Strengths and Virtues: A Handbook and Classification* (American Psychological Association/Oxford University Press, 2004).

As a culture, we seem to have gotten fixated on our weaknesses rather than on our strengths. The culprit is, of course, probably that old negativity bias.

Until very recently, medicine and psychology, for understandable reasons, have tended to focus on how we can fix things that go wrong for people rather than on how we can help them to thrive and flourish—and not get sick in the first place.

For decades, many companies have worked on the unconscious assumption that part of the responsibility of a manager is to try to mitigate the worst effects of their workers' built-in deficiencies and weaknesses. After all, many managers end up becoming managers because they are effective problem solvers, and the people they manage are walking bags of problems—weaknesses—that are ripe for the solving.

When people were encouraged to make greater use of their core strengths at work, they developed a greater passion for their work, and this in turn led to a greater sense of well-being and better work performance.

But today, we are waking up to the exciting realization that people in the workplace are not defective machines that need fixing. Instead, we now know that when we help people understand their talents, and encourage them to focus on doing things that best leverage those talents, they become happier, more fulfilled, and importantly, more productive. When we start to embrace this way of thinking, we are able to take the first step toward sparking a raging inferno of Blue Flames within our team.

IN CASE YOU MISSED IT: THE KEY IDEAS

Negative Nancy: Human evolution caused us to become hyperaware of threats. This wired our brain for something called negativity bias, which makes it easy to get fixated on weaknesses, negative thoughts, and threats. But in the modern world, where the threat of saber-toothed tigers is far less common nowadays, this negativity bias is an unproductive relic—one that can have real consequences in the workplace.

Positive Psychology Emerges: Psychologists realized they were spending too much time focusing on *fixing what is wrong* in people, and missing the chance to help *enhance what is right*. The field of positive psychology emerged, which teaches us leaders that when we spend too much time focused on what we don't do well, we tend to lose sight of where our unique brilliance lies. Instead, this new way of thinking encourages us to discover and lean into our talents.

Don't Get It Twisted: Talents, knowledge, and skills are three distinct, but related, concepts. A *talent* is "a recurring pattern of thought, feeling, or behavior." It's something that tends to show up for you time and time again, in different contexts and situations. *Skills* are proficiencies that can be learned. *Knowledge* consists of things that you know based on factual understanding or experience.

The Results Are In: There is a growing body of research that supports the idea that working *with* our talents—identifying them and using them in our lives and at work—makes us happier, more fulfilled, more energized, and more successful.

You're the Leader, So Lead: For leaders, a key part of our responsibility is to translate the unique talents of those on our team into great results. The best way to turn talent into performance is to put people in roles where their unique talents are utilized, challenged, and strengthened.

CHAPTER 5

Discovering Our Talents

"Everybody has talent. It's just a matter of moving around until you've discovered what it is."

— **George Lucas**

One of America's most recognizable and stylish fast-food barons, Colonel Harland Sanders, was fired from a dozen jobs before he franchised his secret recipe for "Kentucky Fried Chicken" for the first time at age 62. Before that, he was a life insurance salesman, a lawyer, and a ferry boat operator.

World-famous fashion designer Vera Wang pursued careers as a figure skater and a journalist before she first tried her hand at designing a wedding dress—her own. A year later, she opened a small boutique and began designing bridalwear at age forty, and the rest is history. Wang went on to become arguably the most illustrious and successful bridalwear designer in the world.

Sara Blakely, founder of lifestyle brand Spanx, began her career as a Chipmunk at Disney World, failed her LSAT twice, and sold fax machines door-to-door before she realized that she could apply her talent and skill for selling in a way that was more fulfilling to her. She recalled in an interview: "I knew I was good at selling and that I eventually wanted to be self-employed. I thought, instead of fax machines, I'd love to sell something that I created and actually care about."

These examples illustrate that discovering what you can do best can take time, and as George Lucas said, it requires "moving around."

Here is a way to think about the process of discovering and steering yourself toward your talents.

When we are young, life stretches out before us like an expansive twenty-lane highway. Picture, if you can, the city of Houston's famed Katy Freeway, which boasts a whopping twenty-six lanes in certain parts. Like this stretch of Interstate 10, early on, life is a vast and wide-open road to explore.

Sure, each of us is born into a different environment, and has access to different levels of resources. This means that the guardrails on life's highway might be tighter for some than for others, and our opportunity for exploration more limited. Unfortunately, because our world is constructed in an unequal way, some lanes of the highway may be closed to those who were born into less supportive or advantaged circumstances.

However wide your highway is early on, these early years are the time for exploration, for moving in and out of the different lanes on this expansive road of life: sciences, sports, arts, the outdoors, welding, basket weaving, computer programming, relationships, and so on. It is a time for discovery, and for trying things. For tossing things against the wall and seeing what sticks (metaphorically, and sometimes literally). Neurologically, our brains are especially malleable during these earlier years.

We each start off with certain advantages endowed by our unique genetic brain chemistry. This makes certain lanes of that many-lane highway feel smoother, faster, and lower-drag than others. In my own case, the math and sciences lane felt much faster and smoother than the reading comprehension lane. I traveled in both, but my early seedlings of talent for logical thinking—the X-to-Y-to-Z type of thinking—made the ride much smoother in the math lane than in the American history lane.

It can be difficult to see our talents clearly. Sure, driving in the rutted history lane was a valuable ride at the time, as it helped me to slightly sharpen otherwise dull talents like critical reasoning, and build resilience. My determination to get an A in a subject that came less naturally helped me hone what went on to become very important talents later in life: persistence and grit. But nonetheless, it was a bumpier lane, which led me to rule out the possibility of steering my life toward a career in historical studies.

For most people, a good number of lanes remain open for much of our teens and early twenties, especially for those who have the opportunity for post-secondary education. Sometimes, new lanes open up as college introduces us to entirely new disciplines to explore. When used correctly, high schools and universities can be great playgrounds to help us discover our talents.

But as we grow older, it's sensible to start getting clearer on where we're driving toward, and narrowing down which lanes we're driving in. By then, if we've been lucky, we'll have had lots of opportunities to switch lanes, to see which one allows us to go fastest, which is the smoothest. We'll have a feel for which lanes feel bumpy, and start to learn to move out of those lanes to avoid the potholes. This narrows the amount of road we are interested in navigating and starts steering us toward traveling in the lanes where we feel like we can really put the pedal to the metal—those lanes where our strongest talents lie.

Focusing on our core talents—navigating to the smoothest lanes, the ones where we sense we can really start to motor—gives us the best chance of kicking that virtuous cycle we discussed in the last chapter into gear.

But here's the struggle for many people: it can be difficult to see our talents clearly. (Spoiler alert: This is where *you* come in, leaders!)

Alex Linley, author of *Average to A+,* is another pioneer in strengths-based research. His research highlights the fact that the majority of people—a full two-thirds in Linley's experiments—could not identify what their core strengths were.[15]

Of course, if we don't know what our talents are, it is impossible to focus on using them to their fullest potential.

In order to use our talents, we need to, as the ancient Greek aphorism goes, "know thyself."

---

[15] Alex Linley, *Average to A+: Realising Strengths in Yourself and Others* (CAPP Press, 2008).

In his book, Linley asks a few insightful questions that can help you deepen your understanding of your talents, and help the people you are leading to do the same:

- Is there something you remember you always did when you were a kid, something you liked and were good at that you still do?
- What makes you feel comfortable with yourself and makes you think, "Yeah, this is the real me; this is what I do"?
- Are there certain things that come easily to you—things you seem able to do well without having to try too hard?
- What do you find it easy to concentrate on, maybe for long spells, without drifting off or losing focus?
- Can you think of something that you seemed to learn surprisingly quickly?

These are the types of questions you will have the chance to use with your people as you are having Blue Flame conversations.

These questions are critical because, for many of us, our talents can feel shrouded. We struggle to see ourselves clearly, to recognize our own gifts and strengths. And, if we do catch some inkling of them, we may not embrace them: "Who am I to be talented?"

Herein lies one of the most central and significant responsibilities of a leader: to help our people discover and understand their talents. It is only then that we can work with them to put them to their best use.

LEADERS AS FLAME SPOTTERS

From his shabby 64-square-foot abode, which sat over 8,000 feet above sea level and gave him a 360-degree view of the sprawling Los Padres National Forest, Tom Fusek kept watch. He had a real knack for staying focused and vigilant—two of his core talents—which he put to good use scanning the mountains in an intense and systematic way every fifteen minutes.

Tom was a fire spotter, known affectionately to some as the "freaks on the peaks." For generations, these guardians of our wilderness have been stationed proudly atop some of the highest lookouts.

If we don't know what our talents are, it is impossible to focus on using them to their fullest potential.

At the profession's peak—pardon the pun, but I couldn't help myself—there were over ten thousand fire lookout towers in the US, monoliths soaring several stories above the ridgeline like protectors standing tall over the lush valleys below. Each of these perches was inhabited by fire watchers, the watchdogs of the great outdoors armed with binoculars and a radio, constantly scanning the landscape for any signs of smoke.

Today, fire-watching is a dying profession. Technology like drones and airplanes, and policies that require foresters to let fires burn, have caused many fire watchers to hang up their binoculars for the last time.

But despite their near-extinction, the legacy of flame spotters has a lot to offer leaders like us.

We need to foster a new generation of "freaks on the peaks"—leaders who are constantly scanning their teams, keeping watch for latent and budding talents in our teammates, and always on the lookout for even the faintest blue sparks waiting to be ignited.

But unlike flame spotters, we *want* the fires to break out. When we notice even the faintest spark of talent in our people, our job as leaders is to douse those sparks with gasoline (metaphorically, of course), blast them with oxygen, and watch 'em burn brightly.

Too often, people's talents go undetected, like precious gold buried just beneath the earth's surface. We all miss out as a result.

As someone who has interviewed hundreds of job applicants, I know that slightly befuddled look people often show when faced with the classic interview question, "What are you best at?"

It isn't that these people are dense. The reality is that it can be tough to develop an objective view of what's going on in our own heads, and accurately assess our own level of competence.

Sometimes we recognize that we are good at something, but we *underestimate* our level of excellence. We think, "Well this is easy. Everyone must be good at this."

Other times, we *overestimate* our level of talent. We assess our abilities as greater than they actually are. Like that time I stepped up to the karaoke microphone at the office party to do my rendition of "Born in the U.S.A." I knew what the song sounded like. I could hear Springsteen's voice in my head. So, clearly, I could reproduce that sound, right? How hard could it be?

The painful answer is: harder than it seems.

The cognitive bias that explains this is known as the *Dunning-Kruger Effect*, named after two scientists at Cornell University who investigated people's perceptions of their own competency.

In the Dunning and Kruger study, students were asked to undertake tests in grammar, logic, and humor. They were then asked to assess how they felt they had performed in the tests.

In a nutshell, the students who had performed worst in the tests—the ones who had scored only 12 percent in reality—predicted their score would be a whopping 62 percent.

It's a similar type of (misguided) conviction that had me thinking that my rendition of "Born in the U.S.A." pretty much nailed it, while my poor colleagues were cringing in horror.

As author and organizational psychologist Tasha Eurich put it, "When people are steeped in self-delusion, sometimes they are the last ones to find out."

In direct comparison, the students who scored highest of all, at around 85 percent, significantly *underestimated* their predicted score—though not by such a monster margin. That's a lot like Bruce Springsteen himself thinking that his gig was going just okay, but not that great. But meanwhile, the crowd is going completely nuts.

What is fascinating is that when the students were shown their actual results, the best achievers changed their self-assessment. They recognized that they were better than they had realized they were. Interestingly, the lowest achievers, sadly, did not change their self-assessment. They still thought they were far better than they were in reality.

Dunning and Kruger's main conclusion was that people with a serious lack of skills in any area also often lack the competency to recognize their lack of skills. This helps to explain, in part, why people who know diddly-squat about something can be so infuriatingly insistent that they are right and you are wrong.

In other words, our ignorance can sometimes be invisible to us.

But the main takeaway for us flame-spotting leaders is the other side of the same coin: some talented people have a tendency to underestimate their strengths. This is perhaps the blindspot created by our negativity bias.

It's important to note that this is not just modesty, or even false modesty. It simply doesn't always occur to talented people that they are, objectively, extremely good at certain things. They have normalized their level of competency in their own minds.

One of the primary responsibilities that we have as leaders—and I think one of the most important *and* exciting responsibilities we have—is to seek out a clear understanding of everyone's talents, to help each individual develop a clear understanding of their own talents, and to shine a big, bright spotlight on those talents.

In the January 2020 edition of the *Harvard Business Review*, Tomas Chamorro-Premuzic, chief talent scientist at ManpowerGroup, and Jonathan Kirschner, CEO of a global leadership development and coaching technology firm, put it simply: "The ability to see talent before others see it, to unlock human potential, and find not just the best employee for each role, but also, the best role for each employee, is crucial to running a top-notch team. In short, great managers are also great talent agents."

Talent agents—what a powerful and evocative way to frame the role of a leader.

We must meticulously observe those whom we lead and take note of spikes in enthusiasm or effectiveness. When we notice these spikes, we can ask ourselves and our teammates, "What talents are on display in this moment?"

For instance, I might say, "Johnny, I noticed such remarkable *precision* when you presented your summary of the quarter-in-review yesterday. Your command of the details of what drove the business was impeccable. Did you notice that about yourself? What was going on for you at that moment?" Johnny will then help me understand what this talent looks and feels like to him (which will help him to really internalize and own his strength), and we will together figure out ways to help Johnny lean into this talent even harder.

Great managers are also great talent agents.

Jesuit priest and author John Joseph Powell reminded us of the value in doing this at a human level: "It is an absolute human certainty that no one can know his own beauty or perceive a sense of his own worth until it has been reflected back to him in the mirror of another loving, caring, human being." This is Blue Flame spotting.

★ ★ ★

Like him or not, Bill Belichick, coach of the New England Patriots and one of the winningest in NFL history, is a legendary flame spotter. He's a master of noticing talent and potential in unsuspecting places. He built the Patriots into an offensive powerhouse around late-round draft picks, the "leftovers" of the draft class. Some of the team's most prolific offensive producers in recent years—Tom Brady (sixth round pick), Julian Edelman (seventh round pick), Danny Amendola (undrafted), LeGarrette Blount (undrafted)—are among the most noteworthy examples.

One of the key ingredients to Belichick's success has become his uncanny ability to spot latent talent—talent that may not be obvious to others on the surface—that has the ability to fit well into his offensive system.

One of the greatest opportunities a Blue Flame leader has is learning to *notice*.

Take Patriots wide receiver and punt returner Julian Edelman. Edelman spent his college career at College of San Mateo and Kent State University, both low-tier football schools. A quarterback in college, he set several records as a passer. But undersized and unknown, Edelman was not invited to the NFL Combine, the annual invite-only showcase where NFL prospects have a chance to show their stuff to scouts.

Standing only 5'10", Edelman was way undersized as a quarterback, in a draft class with several great ones. His success in college was discounted because he'd been playing against lower-caliber competition. When it came to getting noticed and drafted, the odds were understandably stacked against him, and he flew well below professional scouts' radar.

But on a whim, the Patriots agreed to attend a private workout with Edelman.

Belichick recalled, "We're not thinking he can play quarterback, so we're like, 'Okay, what would we do with Julian? Is he a receiver? Is he a punt returner? Is he a defensive back? Is he maybe a guy who can play multiple positions in the kicking game?'"

Belichick spotted a few things about Edelman that other scouts seemed to be overlooking. First, Edelman had "an intensity that was hard for [opponents] to handle." He spotted this in a blowout loss that Kent State suffered at the hands of juggernaut Ohio State. Edelman fought tirelessly even as the outmatched Kent State team's deficit widened. Some coaches might have seen this whooping as a blemish on the quarterback's résumé, but Belichick noticed *relentlessness*—a talent—in the undersized quarterback. This relentlessness was key to the offensive culture that the coach was building in New England.

Second, Belichick saw a work ethic unlike few he had seen before. Conversations with his coaches and teammates painted a picture of a leader with a mental toughness and dedication that was unmatched in the Kent State locker room. He was, as his teammate said, "always grinding."

This diligence and devotion went on to make Edelman somewhat of a legend in the Patriots' locker room. Fellow Patriots superbowl hero James White remarked, "That guy works extremely hard. He's the first guy in here and leaves last. He's catching tennis balls at six in the morning. As soon as you step in here as a rookie, you see how hard he works, and the results show."

Despite not having some of the prototypical talents that tended to attract NFL teams at the time, Edelman got scooped up by the Patriots in the 2009 draft. Why? Because Belichick—a black-belt flame spotter—could see clearly the talents that he would be getting in the young rookie, and knew that those could be applied effectively within his system.

This seemingly risky move paid off big-time, as he went on to become one of the key players in three Superbowl seasons for the Patriots, collecting awards like Superbowl MVP and Most Receiving Yards along the way.

Blue Flame spotting is the stuff of great leadership, the type of leadership that gets the best out of people and translates it into extraordinary results. And one of the greatest opportunities a Blue Flame leader has is learning to *notice*. To simply notice. Noticing what energizes the people in your charge (and what doesn't). Noticing when they are at their best. And noticing the underlying talents that allow them to function at that level.

When we do this as leaders, it puts us in a position to then put our teammates' talents to their best use.

IN CASE YOU MISSED IT: THE KEY IDEAS

Our Mirrors Are Foggy: Like precious gems hidden just beneath the surface of the ground, it can be difficult to spot and uncover our own talents. A full two-thirds of the subjects in researcher Alex Linley's studies *could not identify what their core strengths were.*

Seeing Ourselves (Un)clearly: Thanks to faulty wiring in our brains—including a cognitive bias known as the Dunning-Kruger Effect—humans are often blind to our talents because it is not easy to accurately assess our own level of competence. As a result, talented people tend to underestimate their talents, which compromises their ability to put them to good use.

Moving Around: The early years of our lives are prime time for discovery and exploration, which can help us better understand where our talents lie. As George Lucas said, "Everybody has talent. It's just a matter of moving around until you've discovered what it is."

Flame Spotting: Leaders play an important role in helping their employees discover their talents, something I call "Blue Flame spotting." They are constantly on the lookout for the latent talents in the people they work with. Effective leaders excel at the art of "noticing," meticulously observing those they lead for clues that point toward their greatest talents.

CHAPTER 6

But What About Our Weaknesses?

I've been advocating—as I expect you've noticed by now—that we lean into what we can do best. Hard. And as flame-spotting leaders, that we help those we lead to discover their greatest talents, and put them in a position where these talents can be put to good use. As we've seen, when we do that, we set off a chain reaction of good stuff that follows. It leads to greater job performance, greater team performance, and a greater state of overall well-being.

This type of approach has been shown to be considerably more fruitful than obsessing over our weaknesses or trying to "fix" ourselves and others so that we can eventually become adequate—at best—at things that are really not our forte.

This way of thinking requires that we accept, even celebrate, the fact that there are things in life we simply aren't good at. For some of us high-achieving types, who endeavor to be good at everything, this can be a tough pill to swallow. (*Gulp.*)

But who are you trying to kid?

Now that we understand why it is important to focus on our own and our teams' strengths, we need to have a nuanced discussion about how to handle weaknesses. (Cue the ominous music.)

Simply pretending they don't exist is obviously not a good strategy. Living in denial with our heads in the sand can, over time, become internally destructive; and externally, it can sabotage our success. It can make us feel insecure, fragile, self-conscious, and like impostors.

It is also delusional—of course talented people like you and me have weaknesses! The unmatchable management guru Peter Drucker, who was always ahead of his time, highlighted this in his seminal 1967 book, *The Effective Executive*. "The idea that there are 'well-rounded' people," wrote Drucker, "people who have only strengths and no weaknesses, is a prescription for mediocrity if not incompetence. Strong people always have weaknesses too. Where there are peaks there are valleys."

When we acknowledge the universal truth that "where there are peaks, there are valleys," and embrace our own shortcomings, it can make us feel whole, balanced, and human.

Admitting that "I have weaknesses"—try saying it aloud for effect—is kind of like that feeling you got as a kid when you finally fessed up to your parents that you had dinged their shiny new car with your old, rusty bike. It was painful to admit, but once you mustered up the courage to come clean, it was a major relief. You could acknowledge it, deal with it, and move ahead. And let's be real: your parents knew you were to blame for the scratch far earlier than you thought they did—in the same way that the people around us at work tend to sniff out that we're not good at something much sooner than we realize. You're not fooling anyone!

But once we've admitted that we have shortcomings, and have begun to become aware of what they are … then what do we do?

For starters, any argument to simply ignore them in favor of our strengths is, of course, plenty shortsighted and perilous. If you are bad at something that is key to fulfilling your duties at work, ignoring it will cause problems sooner or later.

But as we start to peel back the layers on this question, the discussion of how to deal with our weaknesses becomes rather nuanced. For example, on the one hand, recent advances in brain science have shown us that the brain is malleable, and that talents can be cultivated—or that weaknesses can be improved upon and translated into talents—with intentional practice. On the other hand, we know that if we spend our time trying to become good at everything, it just statistically reduces our chances of being great at anything.

I'll try to help you make sense of it all in this chapter, and give you a framework that can help you make conscious choices about what to do with your weaknesses.

The first step is becoming aware of them, which is easier said than done. Some of our more pesky weaknesses have a way of disguising themselves. To make matters even more complicated, our greatest weaknesses are often the shadow side of our greatest talents. Let's explore where our weaknesses hide.

TOO MUCH OF A GOOD THING

The first stop on the road to discovering our weaknesses takes us right back to where we started: our talents.

We tend to assume that, for any particular talent, more is better. But too much of a good thing can often become counterproductive: like eating too much sugar and the ensuing stomachache and energy crash. In that same vein, a perfectly good talent applied in the wrong context can be equally problematic: like putting sugar into a savory mashed potato recipe—which I once did once by mistaking it for salt. Yuck.

In a large international study involving thousands of managers and executives, leadership researchers Robert Kaiser and Bob Kaplan used employee feedback to test how this "too much of a good thing" idea applies to the workplace. They asked respondents to rate their leaders not on the usual five-point scale, but according to whether leaders were using a particular leadership dimension the right amount, too little, or too much.

Some of our more pesky weaknesses have a way of disguising themselves.

Using strengths featured in the StrengthsFinder—a tool created by the same guys who wrote *First, Break All the Rules*—they found that leaders' individual strengths could turn into problem areas when overplayed. Leaders whose strengths included "Achiever," "Activator," or "Command," for example, were more likely to be judged to be exhibiting "too much" forceful leadership. Leaders whose strengths included "Developer," "Harmony," or "Includer" were found to be doing "too much" enabling.

When it came to their impact on their employees, Kaiser and Kaplan found that "too much" of these leadership behaviors was as counterproductive as "too little," and that "the right amount" produced the best results.

Meticulousness and detail-orientation, for example, when taken to the extreme, can make a manager's team feel like they are being micromanaged. But, clearly, these attributes are important and helpful in good doses, and when applied in the right context.

Courage, when taken to an extreme, can cause a CEO to make reckless decisions. But the right amount—subjective as that might seem—can help leaders to take important calculated risks that require some real chutzpah.

A Socratic leader with a real knack for asking great questions can help their team look at issues and opportunities from new angles and pressure-test their thinking in useful ways. But when unchecked, an onslaught of questions can leave teammates feeling like they're not being trusted. This particular road paved with good intentions is one that I have walked on before.

You get the idea. If taken too far, an overreliance on one's strengths—a constant doubling down on the talents that most define us—can result in lopsided leadership. And, in some cases, it can be career-threatening.

One place our weaknesses can be found is on the underside of our talents.

In 1997, Doug Ivester was promoted from CFO of Coca-Cola to its chairman and CEO. He had risen quickly through the ranks, once the youngest vice president ever anointed at the company. As CFO, the self-described man of "substance over style" crushed it and earned the board's confidence. His fact-based, data-driven style coupled with his sharp eye for detail were soaring strengths in his financial leadership role.

But as he stepped into the CEO post, in a classic case of "what got you here won't get you there," Ivester failed to adapt his style. Instead, he continued to call on the things that had made him successful until that point.

His data-driven approach gave short shrift to the importance of human judgment and intuition. His bias for data and facts, which are major assets in the CFO post, caused him to respond objectively and unemotionally (read: coldly) to a safety recall that Coca-Cola faced in Belgium in 1999. What the situation really called for was empathy and understanding—"We messed up. We understand how we disappointed you, and we're really sorry."

Ivester's focus on operating with rigid control systems kept him bogged down in the minutiae of the business as CEO, which meant that the company quickly lost sight of the bigger picture. This became especially problematic at a time when Coca-Cola's business was facing mounting competitive and economic pressures.

Ivester's CEO tenure ended two short years later.

A common area where this "too much of a good thing" challenge shows up is among the striving achiever types for whom *ambition* is a signature strength.

Some of you may be able to relate—I know I sure can.

Achiever types are driven by a constant need for productivity, progress, and attainment. They are constantly seeking to do more, achieve more, and be better. These are, in ways, useful traits when it comes to being a great leader, but what is the shadow side of these good intentions? Do you know the tipping point beyond which this ambition talent can flip to weakness, even becoming a massive liability?

Part of the shadow side of ambition is perfectionism. The ambitious perfectionist will work tirelessly at something until they think it is perfect, which is a fool's errand given that in almost all cases, "perfect" is a mirage. This creates a whole host of potential issues. It can be stressful for the perfectionist ("Ahhhh, I just wish I could get this to be perfect!"), can slow progress ("We can't ship it until it is absolutely *perfect*."), and can frustrate their team ("Your work is never good enough!").

Psychotherapist Robin Farber points out that "perfectionists are driven by a perfect outcome as a way to seek temporary emotional relief from a painful feeling. Perfectionists find it difficult to enjoy the small wins along life's journey, which can take a toll on the individual, the team, and the organization." Perfectionism is often motivated by fear, not by possibility—which is not an empowering place for leaders to be operating from.

A twenty-five-year study by researchers Thomas Curran and Andrew Hill found that today's mounting social pressures are resulting in an alarming rise in perfectionism. They found that as many as two in five children demonstrate perfectionist tendencies. And there is a major cost. In writing about Curran and Hill's research, journalist Amanda Ruggeri concluded that "the rise in perfectionism doesn't mean each generation is becoming more accomplished. It means we're getting sicker, sadder, and even undermining our own potential."[16]

As the ambition/perfectionism duality shows us, the punch line here is that one place our weaknesses can be found is on the underside of our talents that we discussed earlier. They can be two sides of the same coin.

But having a high-fidelity, 360-degree view of ourselves—weaknesses and all—requires that we peel back the layers even farther.

---

[16] Amanda Ruggeri, "The Dangerous Downsides of Perfectionism," BBC Future, February 20, 2018, https://www.bbc.com/future/article/20180219-toxic-perfectionism-is-on-the-rise.

THE IMPORTANCE OF SELF-AWARENESS

Truly understanding our weaknesses (and our talents) usually requires deepening our sense of *self-awareness*. Self-awareness helps us to see ourselves more clearly. It gives us a higher-fidelity view of our strengths and weaknesses. It puts us in a position to more thoughtfully make decisions about where to double down on our greatest strengths, and how to deal with our weaknesses.

Socrates, known as the father of Western philosophy, spoke often about the importance of self-awareness. He coined the idea that "the unexamined life is not worth living." At the time, he was on trial in Athens, and was condemned to death for disturbing the minds of the youth of Athens by his constant questioning of the status quo. If Socrates could not keep examining what he and everyone else knew and could know by means of his constant questioning of accepted beliefs, he said he would rather die—as indeed he did, after being sentenced to kill himself by drinking poisonous hemlock.

We don't need to go that far—and I'm not sure where you'd get hemlock nowadays anyway, Amazon says they're sold out.

But Socrates' wisdom—"the unexamined life is not worth living"—is pure gold for us leaders. As you will learn in just a moment, self-awareness is the cornerstone of being an effective leader, not to mention an effective human being.

To really understand how to deepen our self-awareness, it is important that we slice self-awareness more finely into three parts:

1. Self-knowing: A meta-understanding of ourselves, including knowing who we are, what makes us tick, what we value, and a rounded view of our strengths *and* weaknesses.

2. Momentary self-awareness: A mindfulness about what we are doing, how we are feeling, and what our intentions and motivations are *in this moment*.

3. External self-awareness: Knowing our impact on the people and the world around us. Knowing how other people experience and see us.

Developing self-awareness spanning each of these three dimensions is one of the most important professional meta-skills in today's day and age. Sure, self-awareness has taken on a buzzwordy quality in recent years, but this should not detract from its importance.

A study conducted by Green Peak Partners and Cornell University's School of Industrial and Labor Relations found that, in fact, self-awareness is the interpersonal trait most correlated with leadership success. Researchers reasoned that self-aware leaders are more aware of their own deficiencies, and are more able and willing to "hire to their weaknesses." They also observed that self-aware leaders have the humility "to entertain the idea that someone on their team may have an idea that is even better than their own." Studies have shown that people who see themselves clearly are more promotable, better communicators, better influencers, and ultimately, more effective leaders.

There's also emerging research that is beginning to show that more self-aware CEOs actually lead more profitable companies.

But important as it is, as we began to discuss in the last chapter, seeing ourselves clearly can be tough. Our brains have an unhelpful way of clouding our vision.

LEARNING TO SEE OURSELVES CLEARLY

The late, great NBA player Kobe Bryant, one of the most prolific shooters in NBA history, had a unique and intractable ability to get shots up. Bryant set the record for most shot attempts in a game during the last game of his career, when he shot the ball fifty times to score sixty points for the Lakers. Over his twenty-year career, Bryant took an astounding thirty thousand shots.

This earned Bryant the much-loathed "ball hog" designation among his most vocal critics. But the fifteen-time NBA All-Star embraced the nickname as an unavoidable byproduct of his amazing shooting talent.

"I wouldn't say I'm a ball hog. I'm a shooter," he said. "I don't necessarily hog the ball, but I put them up though. I definitely much rather shoot it than pass it. That's just how I am."

As you can see, it isn't especially difficult for our egos to accept that our amazing talents can actually become problematic. It is considerably easier to admit a "strength overuse" than it is to acknowledge a deficiency—a real deal-breaking, project-wrecking, game-losing humdinger of a weakness.

As we touched on earlier, it can be easy for us humans to slip into denial about having any of such weaknesses. We have brittle egos that make it too threatening to admit any inadequacy, so our egos distort our perception of reality in order to keep us safe.

Look no further than my golf game, which is so bad I had to have my ball retriever regripped. If I didn't have my scorecard to objectively keep me honest about how bad I am, I might be living in denial. After all, admitting that I'm bad at golf might pose a threat to my social standing with my golf buddies—or so I tell myself.

There are real mental barriers to seeing ourselves clearly. Furthermore, our culture often tends to reward overconfidence and arrogance. Look no further than Donald Trump's unexpected presidential victory, or the meteoric rise to fame of Elizabeth Holmes and her now-defunct company, Theranos.

The evidence that self-awareness can be difficult to achieve challenges the assumption that "I know myself best." At some level, this assumption makes logical sense. After all, you are the only person on Earth who has a record of every feeling, experience, win, and loss that *you* have experienced. But in reality, we are—in general—less self-aware than we think.

Case in point: organizational psychologist Tasha Eurich, author of the book *Insight: The Power of Self-Awareness in a Deluded World*, concluded that 95 percent of people think they're self-aware, but only 10 to 15 percent truly are. There is, for most people, significant distortion between how we see ourselves, and how others actually experience us.

Furthermore, I have bad news for all of you senior executives out there: your self-awareness mirror is likely to be foggiest of all. Eurich's research uncovered that there is actually an inverse relationship between power and self-awareness. The most senior executives tend to be the least self-aware compared with leaders who are lower on the org chart. This is, in effect, the reverse Dunning-Kruger effect, where people overestimate their abilities not because of their relative ignorance, but because they are in a position that assumes a certain level of knowledge and skill.

Seniority makes it difficult to see the truth, and much easier to lose touch with it. Power dynamics play a role too: as a senior executive, people are more likely to praise you, agree with you, tell you you're doing well—even if they don't actually feel that way. In many situations, it's easier for people to agree with leadership than it is to tell them the truth about their lame ideas.

"We should make a jump-to-conclusions mat. It's a mat where you jump to conclusions!"

"Good idea, boss!"

Err, not.

As Dutch leadership scholar Manfred Kets De Vries famously quipped, "Leaders are surrounded by walls, mirrors, and liars."

There is, for most people, significant distortion between how we see ourselves, and how others actually experience us.

So we've established that this self-awareness business is hugely important if you want to be effective, but can be really difficult. So how do we fix the disconnect between how the world sees us, and how we see ourselves? Well, a good place to start is to find someone who will tell you the truth about what they see, or as Eurich puts it, "a loving critic." And for leaders, when it comes to your role in helping your people to deepen their own self-awareness, *be* the loving critic.

Heck, why not build a whole network of people who are committed to helping you see what they see? Adam Grant, bestselling author of several leadership books and the top-ranked professor at the Wharton School of the University of Pennsylvania, formed what he calls his "Challenge Network," an alliance of trusted confidants who are so committed to his success that they are willing to give it to him straight.

As an organizational psychologist, Grant understands the Dunning-Kruger effect, and the fact that bias can get in the way of seeing ourselves clearly. "I think the big lesson here is that any time a trait is easy for other people to see or hard for us to admit, we can't trust our own judgment of it."

So, find someone (or several someones) you trust and enroll them in your Challenge Network:

"Cheryl, I want to be a better teammate to you, and an important part of that is to more clearly understand where my trusted teammates like you see me succeeding, and also where you see me failing or under-delivering. So I really need your honest take, and you can be totally candid with me ... I can take it. I want to grow and get better!"

Then listen to their feedback with ears and heart open. In many ways, your success depends on it.

DEALING WITH OUR WEAKNESSES

As we develop a clearer sense of our weaknesses, that of course brings up the question: what do we do with them?

Self-help culture is littered with well-intentioned but potentially problematic advice on the matter.

For example, we're told, "You can do anything that you set your mind to," leaving us to believe that even the most pernicious weaknesses can be overcome and that with the right amount of hard work, we can evolve into perfectly balanced all-arounders, people who are equally good at everything.

It is easy to buy into this idea because it feels good. And companies can slip into this trap too, thinking that with the right amount of manager training, mentorship programs, and expensive weekend seminars, they can develop these perfectly well-rounded unicorn supermanagers.

"We'll just make a bunch of these good-at-everything supermanagers, and all of our problems will be solved," we can sometimes trick ourselves into thinking. Instead of spending time to guide managers to positions where their talents can be best leveraged and further strengthened, they put together complicated twenty-point leadership competency frameworks that they work diligently to help these leaders-of-the-future conform to.

We can imagine the perfectly balanced leader. One minute she's jumping to the podium to deliver a rousing, impassioned company address, setting out her view of the company's growth strategy, and inspiring us all with the brilliance of her vision for what's possible. The crowd goes wild.

The next minute, she's sharing a trying personal story with a small group, captivating us with her vulnerability and authenticity. Perhaps it's the one about how she had to resit one course in psychoneuroimmunology before being awarded her degree in neuroscience and moving on to Stanford for her MBA. "I've accepted now that I can't be absolutely brilliant at absolutely everything, absolutely all of the time. It makes me feel very humble."

She breaks off the conversation only when she is called to an impromptu press conference. She picks off each and every question with sharpshooting precision, with just the right statistic at the ready to prove that the organization is on track to smash all of its targets.

She is speedy, yet comprehensive. Tough, yet vulnerable. Analytical, but able to deal in abstractions. Big-picture, but knows the details. Enterprising and risk-taking, yet able to mitigate risk. Planful, yet nimble.

You get the picture.

Make no mistake about it, I commend well-intentioned organizations who actively develop and grow their leaders and help them to strengthen new leadership muscles. This is important.

The trouble is, these supermanagers—the "ten out of ten across-the-board" types—don't exist. And people who strive for this aren't as effective as they are cracked up to be.

As we start to see our weaknesses more clearly, it can be tempting to want to mobilize quickly against them, especially if we haven't yet accepted that it is, in fact, okay to suck at some things. (You achiever types probably catch my drift.) But before you go hastily click "Buy Now" on a book series that can help you to improve your newly discovered weakness, you may want to hang tight. Endeavoring to become good at everything as your default response to weakness can come at a cost.

Instead of defaulting to trying to fix all of your weaknesses, let me suggest a more practical, conscious approach.

Once we have identified our weaknesses, we have three basic options that we can make a conscious choice from: **we can endeavor to strengthen them, mitigate them, or ignore them.**

Strengthen   Mitigate   Ignore

STRENGTHEN THEM

I once worked with an amazing entrepreneur, Mark, who had founded and built a very successful, innovative software business. Mark was a talented technologist and business leader, but he had a deep, dark secret: he was dreadful with numbers.

It wasn't exactly a case of dyscalculia or number blindness; it was more the "I was never great at math, so I've just avoided it" sort of ineptitude.

Before we go any further, this is a good time to point back to the earlier distinction we drew between *skills* and *talents*. Skills are proficiencies that can be learned—like a surgeon learning how to make the perfect incision. By contrast, we can think of talents as recurring patterns of behavior upon which skills can be built. In the case of the same surgeon, he or she needs some degree of talent in the manual dexterity department in order to build the incision-making skill. It's not especially surprising, therefore, that many great surgeons are also musicians, applying that same underlying talent of manual dexterity to a different skill like playing the piano.

In Mark's case, he hadn't yet built the *skill* or pattern recognition needed to more completely understand financial statements. But Mark had gobs of *talent* in a few key areas that lent themselves well to developing financial literacy.

First off, Mark was *analytical*; an engineer from an early age, he made his fortune writing software using a similar type of sequential logic as is required to read financial statements. Mark's brain was also very *contextual*, lending him a strong ability to make sense of one thing—in the case of financial statements, a month of performance—in the context of a broader pattern or history.

It turns out "not being good with numbers" wasn't the heart of Mark's problem.

Rather, from early on, Mark was just never that interested in accounting. Not being interested caused him to avoid developing the skill, which kept him disinterested because he wasn't good at it. Remember the virtuous cycle we discussed earlier in the talents section? The same cycle can work in reverse—as a *vicious* cycle—keeping us bad at things that we're not interested in because we avoid doing them.

Nevertheless, over time, Mark developed a strong intuitive grasp of where his business stood financially, but when he looked at a financial spreadsheet, his eyes still glazed over. He understood what was going on in the business, but had a poor grasp on the finer details of the numbers.

As Mark saw it, if he focused on building a great product, the numbers stuff would take care of itself.

He coped for years by leaning heavily on his finance guys. He made sure that every management report came with commentary that told him all the figures he needed to know. He pretended to look at the spreadsheets and could pick out a few figures that seemed to tally with the top-line numbers, so he assumed all was well. As for the quarterly and annual reports that he owed to investors—"Hey, that's what the numbers guys are for."

But as the business grew, Mark began to worry that he might be missing something significant and was feeling increasingly uncomfortable about relying entirely on his finance director.

When Mark finally confessed that this was becoming a problem, he and I set a plan in motion. I asked Mark to get together with his finance director and pluck up the courage to fess up to him too. Mark wasn't keen on this idea because he felt it would undermine his authority. But we talked it through some more and Mark came to agree that what posed an even bigger potential risk to his authority was some unforeseen financial misstep he should have caught, in which case he'd be forced to admit he didn't understand the numbers in a much less favorable light.

He approached Alan, his finance director, and came clean. Alan, a competent and kind-hearted fella, was less than astonished by the news. Without Mark having to ask, Alan volunteered to spend time with Mark to help him graduate beyond a 101-level understanding of the financials. Every month-end financial review meeting became a crash course and a learning opportunity.

Guess what? Mark got better at finance. He became competent pretty quickly. How? He built this new skill on a foundation of applicable, preexisting talents.

This is an important point to park on for a moment:

It is considerably easier to build new *skills* if the right foundational *talents* are in place.

Someone who is inherently detailed and meticulous—who dots i's, crosses t's, and can't sleep until everything in their house is in its right place—will find it considerably easier to learn accounting than someone whose signature strength is, for example, abstraction.

Similarly, you're way likelier to become good at dancing—a skill—if you are innately rhythmic and physically graceful, than if you have cloth ears and two left feet.

But what about developing new *talents*?

Advances in brain science give us hope. Neuroscience has taught us a lot about the capacity for the brain to rewire itself—literally changing its structures and pathways—in response to learning and experience. The brain can, in fact, grow and adapt with the right exercise. This idea has become known as "neuroplasticity."

Findings in this area have shown that neurogenesis—the production of new neurons—can continue throughout the human life span. The formation of new neural pathways usually happens in response to some stimulus, like having new thoughts or learning new skills. Repetition and practice strengthen these pathways, while the lesser-used pathways deteriorate and weaken, as is the case with our muscles.

Here's the catch: although neurogenesis can happen throughout the human life span—beyond just the usual childhood developmental period—the rate of potential change declines as we age. It is still possible to develop new talents as we age, but it becomes more difficult. It is tougher—though not impossible, as the brain science tells us—to teach an older dog new tricks.

★ ★ ★

In 2005, freelance journalist Joshua Foer was covering the USA Memory Championship, a rather odd event where memory nerds from across the states—"widely varying in both age and hygienic upkeep," per Foer—compete in contests such as memorizing decks of playing cards, long strings of numbers, and poems.

His first exposure to the world of memory competition left Foer dumbstruck. "My own memory was average at best," he wrote. "Among the things I regularly forgot: where I put my car keys; the food in the oven; my girlfriend's birthday; our anniversary; Valentine's Day ..." and the list went on. By contrast, these memory athletes, like then-reigning World Memory Champion Ben Pridmore, could memorize the order of an entire shuffled deck of playing cards in under a minute.

Foer assumed that these must be intellectual freaks of nature, prodigious savants born with the incredible gift of superior cognition.

But then he met Ed Cooke, a curly-haired British mnemonist who had entered the US competition as a training run for the upcoming World Memory Championships. When Foer asked Cooke when he first realized he was a savant, Cooke chuckled. "Oh, I'm not a savant," he said. "My memory is quite average. All of us here have average memories."

Fascinated by his distinct blend of impeccable recall, sharp wit, and lighthearted playfulness, Foer went on to strike up a friendship with Cooke. During an evening of drinking together after the New York contest—during which Foer learned that memory skills can evidently make for great bar tricks—Cooke gave Foer a window into the techniques that memory athletes use to perform such seemingly impossible feats. Superior memory, Cooke professed, wasn't a matter of genetic privilege or innate neurological advantage. Rather, it was a matter of learning new ways of storing information in your brain so that you can remember more. Cooke insisted anyone could do it, if they were willing to put in the practice.

Cooke was so committed to proving his point that he offered to take Foer—who confessed to having a Swiss cheese memory and often being incapable of remembering what he had eaten for breakfast—under his wing. "I reckon you could win the championships next year with an hour's practice a day," said Cooke.

Foer agreed. He was skeptical, but committed. "I couldn't help but think that it would make me more persuasive, more confident, and, in some fundamental sense, smarter," he wrote. "Certainly I'd be a better journalist, friend, and boyfriend. But more than that, I imagined that having a memory like [World Memory Champion] Ben Pridmore's would make me an altogether more attentive, perhaps even wiser, person."

Under Cooke's tutelage, Foer learned and mastered memory techniques like the memory palace—an ancient technique where vivid images are linked to objects (cards, pictures, etc.) to be memorized and stored in physical locations envisioned by the mind.

One year later, Foer—who months later still struggled to remember what he'd had for lunch on a given day—went on to become the 2006 USA Memory Champion!

As Mark and Joshua's stories teach us, we *can* get smarter, better, or more skilled at things outside of our signature strengths, even later in life. And especially if the underlying talents are there.

But it takes deliberate, often intense, practice, which comes at the cost of time.

The decision of whether to invest in shoring up a weakness comes down to this: if we choose to spend time strengthening areas that don't come as naturally, we lose time we could otherwise be spending leveraging what we do best. This is a trade-off we must closely consider.

Some weaknesses we struggle with are less a result of talent deficiency, but rather, stem from a self-imposed limitation, a belief that needs reframing, or a mental roadblock on an otherwise fast and smooth lane on our talent highway.

There is almost always more to the story than just "not being good at it."

For example, if you struggle to approach potentially valuable business contacts at a conference, it could stem from a fear that you'll get rejected rather than a total lack of the needed social skills. In a similar way, challenges that an otherwise competent communicator may have with public speaking could stem from a fear that they will flub.

Mark's struggles with understanding the financials probably stemmed, in part, from a fear that he didn't *entirely* get this numbers stuff and wanted to avoid being shown up. Mark likes to be extremely good at anything he takes on, which was getting in the way of his learning to be merely competent.

It's important to become aware of and examine self-defeating stories or patterns like these, ones that may be at the heart of what's holding you back—as opposed to some massive talent deficiency.

> **ACTIONABLE: WHAT TO DO WITH WEAKNESSES**
>
> You can improve and build new talents, but you should think carefully about the trade-offs between focusing on using your talents and strengthening your weaknesses. Developing new talents requires time and deliberate practice, and there are only so many hours in a day. Are your hours better spent applying the things that you can do best, or building up the things that you can't?
>
> Only you can decide. When faced with this choice, or when you are counseling someone on your team who is at the same fork in the road, here are a few questions to ask:
>
> - Is my weakness preventing me from achieving something I aspire to?
> - Does that weakness come at a cost that is unacceptable to me?
> - Is the weakness a *skill* I've simply yet to develop, or an underlying *talent* that isn't part of my repertoire already?
> - Can I acquire that new skill by investing an amount of time and energy that I am comfortable with? Will that investment be worth it?

MITIGATE THEM

We talked earlier about identifying and focusing on a team member's strengths and "managing around" their weaknesses, but that's not the same thing as simply ignoring weaknesses. When it comes to developing strategies that can help you minimize or eliminate the negative consequences of things you are not as good at, the primary strategy I'll offer is to team up with people who complement you.

Kiara was a cofounder and CTO of a successful software company. She had a few signature talents that stood out—an ability to deeply *focus*, and an ability to *envision* and *create* things—which fueled her obsession with conceiving and cranking away at new product ideas. When she had an idea, she would plug away at it day and night. She once had a vision for a prototype of a product extension and holed up in her office for a full week hammering away at it—despite the fact that the module was not on the product road map.

> **If we choose to spend time strengthening areas that don't come as naturally, we lose time we could otherwise be spending leveraging what we do best.**

In the company's early stages, the market success of their beta product proved that there could be a pot of gold at the bottom of some of Kiara's rabbit holes. But as the business achieved product market fit and developed a more robust product road map, the company needed her to forget about her hobbyhorse for the time being, and stay focused on the agreed-to business priorities that were most critical to bringing home the bacon. One of those priorities was providing clear and focused leadership to the product and engineering teams in her charge, something she often lost sight of as she was dreaming up and cranking away at new ideas.

This became a real issue for the business. Kiara's development team was regularly missing deadlines. They felt whiplashed by the constantly shifting priorities as they sprinted from shiny object to shiny object. The company was missing customer commitments and developing a reputation in the market for being slow to offer new releases.

Kiara's CEO, an exemplary Blue Flame spotter himself, had an idea: let's get the most out of Kiara's talents by repositioning her role to focus on her towering strengths. They would make her chief engineer. She could have the greatest impact if they let her build products—that was what she was most talented at and most passionate about.

Then, he decided to partner her with a top-notch product leader with strength in agile product management and an arsenal of team leadership, collaborative, and executional talents. This person would ensure that the team was operating with the discipline and focus required to stay on track with delivery deadlines, something Kiara wasn't inclined to do as she got head-deep into an exciting product enhancement.

Teaming these two up went on to work out marvelously.

There are plenty of famous examples of dynamic duos whose talents complement one another, like peanut butter and jelly. People whose strengths help to offset the other's struggles.

At Facebook, Mark Zuckerberg brought the visionary and technical talents, while Sheryl Sandberg brought the leadership and executional skills. A world away, in a castle made of ice cream, Ben brought the marketing and operational chops while Jerry brought a genius for making great-tasting ice cream. Deep in an FBI basement somewhere, Scully is objective and fact-based while Special Agent Mulder is intuitive and abstract. These dynamic duos are far more powerful together than either of them would be on their own.

When we have recognized that a particular weakness has the potential to blunt our effectiveness, and if it seems too deep-rooted for us to be able to *improve* on it, then the next option is to use strategies to *mitigate* it.

And the best way to do that, in general, is to team up with someone, or several someones, whose strengths complement your own. Find someone who supplies the yin to your yang. The Ben to your Jerry. Or the Mulder to your Scully. Craft your respective roles in such a way that has them focused on doing what they can do best, and you focused on what you can do best.

IGNORE THEM

While it's totally counter to so much self-help these days, and ultimate heresy to the "we have to fix our weaknesses" orthodoxy, maybe, just maybe, you can *ignore* your weaknesses. When we embrace and work with people's strengths, we have to recognize that there will be other areas in which they are relatively weak. But some weaknesses, it turns out, actually don't matter that much in certain contexts.

Remember the fallacy about the well-rounded leader? As you know by now, our efforts are much better applied in leveraging strengths rather than focusing on weaknesses. And if it's not incredibly detrimental to your business or ability to lead, don't worry about your weakness; you're human

By thinking about the talents and skills needed to succeed in your role, and comparing those to your own self-assessment, you will start to get clear which ones you really need to work on sharpening, which need to be somehow mitigated, and which can be largely ignored.

Team up with someone, or several someones, whose strengths complement your own.

I'll give you a personal example: I've discovered from a few home DIY projects that I am very bad at visualizing things in three dimensions. This is oddly specific, I know. If I am trying to cut a piece of timber to make even a simple 45-degree joint, I'm fine only so long as I can see both bits of timber lined up in the correct place. Pick up one piece of timber, flip it over, and hand it back to me, and I will invariably make the cut with the wrong slope. I struggle to visualize what shape it should be once it is spun back around. Or over? Or whatever. You see the problem?

In most contexts within my work life, this is a weakness I can let go of. No one—even the more engineering-focused companies I have worked with—is going to ask me to do any serious 3D modeling anytime soon, and if they tried, I probably wouldn't trust them anymore.

There are talents that we lack that are simply not mission-critical to the role we are playing, the goals we aspire to achieve, and the impact that we are trying to have on the world. Let those go.

IN CASE YOU MISSED IT: THE KEY IDEAS

Clean Your Lenses: With all this talk of leaning into our strengths, what about our weaknesses? What do we do with those? First, we must see them and understand them.

Our Mirrors Get Foggy: It is easy for us humans to slip into denial about our weaknesses, especially for those of us in power. Subconsciously, our brittle egos think it's threatening to acknowledge an inadequacy, so our egos distort our perception when it comes to things we're not good at. As a result, we are, on average, less self-aware than we think. There tends to be significant distortion between how we see ourselves, and how others actually experience us.

Self-Awareness Is Key: Seeing ourselves clearly, developing a 20/20 vision of our strengths and weaknesses, and working from that understanding is the cornerstone of being an effective leader. It helps us to more thoughtfully make decisions about where to double down on our greatest strengths and how to deal with the things that come less naturally. It helps us to ensure that we are able to get the best of our talents, while mitigating their inevitable shadow sides.

Find Loving Critics: In order to deepen your self-awareness, find people who will tell you the truth about how they see you. Find someone who cares so much about you and your success and well-being that they're willing to give it to you straight. Compare their feedback to your own self-understanding. This can help you to deepen your understanding of yourself, and how others see you.

Blessing and a Curse: Sometimes, it turns out, it is the shadow side of our greatest talents that can create the greatest liabilities. As a leader, your talent can turn into a problem when it's overplayed. If you lean on your talent too hard, or in the wrong context, it can result in lopsided leadership. and in some cases, it can be career-threatening.

Making a Choice: As we develop a clearer sense for our weaknesses, we have three basic alternatives when it comes to what to do with them: we can endeavor to strengthen them, we can mitigate them, or we can simply ignore them.

Two Roads Diverged: Research shows that with deliberate, sustained effort and practice, we can build new skills and talents. But developing new talents requires time and deliberate practice, and there are only so many hours in a day. Are your hours better spent applying the things that you can do best, or building up the things that you can't?

Hey, it's Dan here. I'm the book's author.

I hope you're enjoying it so far, and finding it enlightening, practical, and fun! I have a favor to ask you. Would you consider giving the book a rating on Amazon, please? My goal for this book is to help as many leaders as I can to bring out the best in their people, and a boatload of Amazon love can really help in that mission.

Many thanks in advance,

— **Dan**

Dan Cremons

PART 03

Passions: Do What Most Invigorates You

CHAPTER 7

What Makes You Come Alive?

> "Don't ask yourself what the world needs. Ask yourself what makes you come alive, and go do that, because what the world needs is people who have come alive."
>
> — **Howard Thurman**

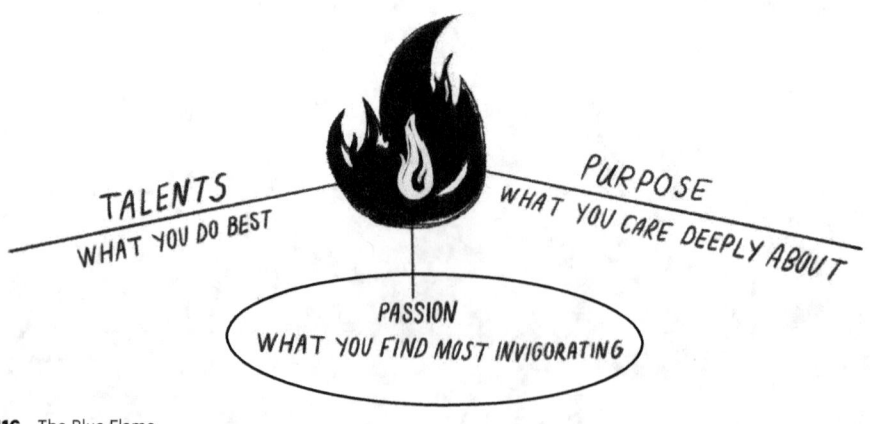

I used to love watching *The Drew Carey Show* in the 1990s. I can recall an especially amusing moment when Carey is sarcastically egging on his dejected, Eeyorish coworker as she is carrying on about how much she loathes her job.

"Oh, you hate your job?" Drew asks. "Why didn't you say so? There's a support group for that. It's called *everybody*, and they meet at the bar."

Work is an easy target for funny-because-it's-true satire of this sort. Because the reality is, many people aren't happy with their job. A paltry 13 percent of people are truly passionate about their work.[17]

But it has been well-established—through extensive research, our own everyday experiences, and a bit of common sense—that we perform considerably better when we are lit up by the work we're doing. When we, as civil rights leader Howard Thurman put it, have "come alive," our output is more creative, higher quality, and more impactful. Best of all, we enjoy the process way more.

Research by Harvard Business School professor Jon M. Jachimowicz points to one contributing factor that's creating this gap: many—if not most—of us don't know how to go about finding and pursuing what lights us up. So we end up leaving our potential sitting on the shelf, collecting dust like a limited-edition Blu-ray of *Titanic*.

Blue Flame leaders play a vital role in changing this paradigm—in helping our people discover what will truly make them come alive.

---

[17] "Deloitte Study: Only 13 Percent of the US Workforce Is Passionate About Their Jobs," Deloitte, June 7, 2017, https://www.prnewswire.com/news-releases/deloitte-study-only-13-percent-of-the-us-workforce-is-passionate-about-their-jobs-300469952.html.

"Follow your passion" has become a delicious cliché in American culture, one that armchair career counselors and gurus everywhere have peddled for years. Its virtues have been littered throughout a vast sea of self-help literature. It has become the centerpiece of countless commencement addresses and keynote speeches, and one of the hackneyed platitudes posterized on the walls of corporate America.

It is no surprise, nor a crime, that this advice is dispensed so frequently. After all, it is positive and can feel very empowering. But it has become so hyperbolic that it runs the risk of going in one ear and out the other. Though it fits nicely in a tweet, its simplicity creates more questions than it answers. For example, are we supposed to have just one passion? And should we just keep searching until we have found that thing?

A paltry 13 percent of people are truly passionate about their work.

What if my passion is basketball, but I am 5-foot-nothing, clumsy, and have poor eyesight? Should I leave it all behind to pursue my passion for playing professional ball? Should I follow my passion for switchboard operating, or typewriter repair, even though the need for those professions went away like thirty years ago? Is my greatest passion really going to make for a lucrative career?

Despite the nuances here, which we'll dive into and deconstruct later, the idea of following our passion—clichéd and passé as it may have become—is essential advice. Our families, workplaces, and communities need people who have come alive—especially now, given the energy crisis we're facing in today's knowledge economy.

British author Sir Ken Robinson, who gave one of the most watched TED talks of all time, is on a new mission to bring attention to the brutal reality facing American enterprises: far too many people are simply working for the weekend. We need to light the workforce up now more than ever if we want our businesses to realize their full potential, and if we want to solve some of the hairy social, environmental, and economic issues that threaten our future.

But Robinson also offers hope that leaders like you and me can change this paradigm by helping our people to find what makes them come alive. He writes:

> "An awful lot of people don't enjoy what they do. They kind of get through the week and wait for the weekend. And there's a lot of evidence for that;

there's been a lot of research to show there are huge levels of disengagement at work. You only have to look at other really startling figures like the growth in the sales of antidepressant drugs and levels of drop-out rate from schools. There's massive evidence around the world of people not getting a lot from their lives and often being angry and frustrated by them. And, yet, I also meet people who absolutely love what they do, who can't wait to get to it. If you were to say to them, "Why don't you try something else for a while?" they really wouldn't know what you're talking about. They'd say, 'Well, this isn't what I do. *This is who I am*.'" [18]

If your company or organization was chock-full of people who "absolutely love what they do, who can't wait to get to it," what might it be capable of?

Helping people find what they "absolutely love to do" starts with helping them to discover and navigate toward their passions.

When we are doing things that feel energizing, even exhilarating, work starts to no longer feel like work.

It was Patagonia founder Yvon Chouinard's early love for falconry that led him to start climbing the rock faces of California. Chouinard, born in 1938, was a leading climber in what is now known as the "Golden Age of Yosemite Climbing." He was part of the team that first scaled the North America Wall of El Capitan without fixed ropes in 1964. The following year, he and a fellow climber made a famous ascent of El Capitan's Muir Wall, helping to establish this style of modern rock climbing, using no advance preparation and limited climbing aids.

When we discover and orient ourselves toward the types of activities we find invigorating, amazing things can happen.

As climbers make their way up a rock face, they hammer flat metal spikes called pitons into crevices in the rock, to which they attach a safety rope. Early pitons were made of soft iron that molded into the crevice, making them almost impossible to remove. Chouinard didn't like the fact that this spoiled the rock face's natural state. So, he

---

[18] Jane Clayson, "Sir Ken Robinson On Discovering Your Passions," *On Point* (WBUR, June 19, 2013), https://www.wbur.org/onpoint/2013/06/19/sir-ken-robinson.

bought a second-hand forge and anvil and began to manufacture hardened steel pitons that could be hammered out of the rock and reused. He eked out a living selling his pitons to fellow climbers from the back of his truck and, over time, developed a successful climbing equipment business, Chouinard Equipment Ltd.

But Chouinard began to feel that even his reusable pitons were causing too much damage to the rock face, spoiling it for future climbers. He devised a new kind of aluminum chock that could be wedged into a crevice, leaving the rock undamaged. He stopped manufacturing his hardened pitons, even though they accounted for most of his company's revenues at the time, and became a leading advocate for what he went on to call "clean climbing." He would say that "how you climb a mountain is more important than reaching the top."

Chouinard has always felt a deep love for "silent sports"—kayaking, fly-fishing, surfing, rock climbing—which bring people into close contact with nature and themselves. Born of his personal passion for the outdoors and his deep-seated belief in the importance of "using business to protect nature," Patagonia grew into a hugely successful outdoor clothing and supplies company.

Until his retirement, Chouinard kept surfboards in the closet at Patagonia headquarters, and could often be seen dipping out for a frolic in the nearby surf with his coworkers. And still today, the company donates 1 percent of its sales or 10 percent of net profit, whichever is greater, to environmental causes that are meaningful to Chouinard and his team.

The origin story of Patagonia teaches us that when we discover and orient ourselves toward the types of activities we find invigorating, amazing things can happen.

IN CASE YOU MISSED IT: THE KEY IDEAS

The Fire Is Fading: Only about 20 percent of workers are truly passionate about their work. Research has shown that this is, in part, because many—if not most—of us don't know how to go about finding and pursuing what lights us up. And as a result, we fail to do so, leaving a lot on the table in the process.

Be the Change: Leaders like you and me can change this paradigm by helping our people to find the types of things that make them come alive. The key is to push them to discover and navigate toward the types of *activities that invigorate them*. When we are doing things that feel energizing, even exhilarating, work starts to no longer feel like work.

What's Possible? Start by asking yourself: if my company or organization was chock-full of people who *"absolutely love what they do, who can't wait to get to it,"* what might we be capable of achieving?

CHAPTER 8

Discover What Invigorates You

"The best moments in our lives are not the passive, receptive, relaxing times ... The best moments usually occur if a person's body or mind is stretched to its limits in a voluntary effort to accomplish something difficult and worthwhile."

— **Mihaly Csikszentmihalyi**

Think of an activity in your life that keeps drawing you back, one that puts you totally "in the zone." You love it. It stirs your soul. You become totally immersed in it. It is, in a word, *invigorating*.

For a long time, playing music has had this sort of effect on me. From a young age, I had a knack for fiddling around on instruments and creating music, which I suppose sprouted from some amount of natural talent, some inborn ability to discern pitch, rhythm, timbre, and tone. Although, to be fair, at a young age this "music" was more like squeaks, creaks, and clanks, the sorts of sounds you would imagine a dying wildebeest makes.

I recall a moment in fourth-grade music class when, during a lesson on the basics of notes and chords, Miss Delaney keyed a chord on the piano, outside of her students' line of sight—many of whom were picking their nose or making paper airplanes.

"Does anyone know what that is called?" she asked.

"A G-major triad," I retorted, oblivious to the fact that Miss Delaney—who by the looks of it, was awestruck by my reply—was looking for a far more rudimentary answer, like "a chord."

The next year, when Miss Delaney sent us home with recorders (you know, the parental torture devices disguised as little plastic wind instruments), I had that thing pretty well figured out within a couple of days. Although, it took me a few more to master what I thought would be a fifth-grade fan favorite, "Total Eclipse of the Heart." Much to my surprise, this didn't raise my cool quotient much.

As time went on, I leaned into music wholeheartedly. It drew me in. Something about the ability to create something from nothing really got me going. I came to love the challenge of learning new instruments, genres, songs, and theories. I relished any chance I could find to collaborate and make music with other musicians. I couldn't get enough of the seductive smell of spruce and mahogany at the local guitar shop—a scent that years later I would be forced to explain to my wife when I came back home after a day of "running errands."

The little seedlings of musical talent that I was endowed with early began to sprout as my passion for music took hold. With practice, I continued to get better, which further deepened my interest. It is that virtuous cycle we learned about back in Chapter 4.

I went on to pay my rent through college by playing weekend gigs at musty bars and restaurants with a few local acts. The tips were decent, and the free drinks were a nice perk for a poor college kid. But what kept me coming back was *"that moment."* Its recollection alone gives me a tingly feeling, one of vitality and aliveness.

I can find "that moment" in a variety of places. I found it within the fandango-style dual guitar section of a "Hotel California" cover. I found it during that rad bass intro leading into a cover of "Sweet Child O' Mine." I found it during a rip-roaring improvisation on the tail end of a Def Leppard cover. In these moments, I find myself completely engrossed in the music. Time feels suspended. Despite being hyperaware of the present moment, my brain switches off and my intuition runs the show. I feel simultaneously at ease, alert, energized, and challenged—but confident.

It is, well, *invigorating*.

We talked in Chapter 4 about psychologists Mihaly Csikszentmihalyi and Martin Seligman, pioneers of the positive psychology movement and about how Csikszentmihalyi coined and popularized the term *flow* to describe this state of pure absorption and enjoyment.

Growing up in World War II–ravaged Italy, where the ground frequently shook as bombs rained down on Rome, Csikszentmihalyi—who goes by "Mike" to keep it easy—had a far from idyllic childhood. However, amid the tragedy and turmoil of war, he learned early on that taking up interesting activities—like chess—could provide a temporary distraction from the stress of the outside world. It was an important coping mechanism.

When he was playing chess, "it didn't bother [him] that bombs were exploding." Csikszentmihalyi recalls that "it was one of the first times I realized you could get taken up in something to the point where everyday life problems disappeared, at least temporarily." This was a close-to-home lesson in the power of what he later went on to describe as "flow."

In the wake of the war's destruction, Csikszentmihalyi noticed adults around him wearily grappling with the tragedies that had befallen them. They struggled to rebuild their lives and regain their identities. Many had understandably lost the will to try after enduring significant loss, experiencing unspeakable atrocities, and living in terrible conditions as refugees. He became fixated on a question that few children would think to ponder: *what makes life worth living?*

Through his teenage and early adult years, Mike was (and still is) a seeker. He looked through the prisms of philosophy, art, religion, and science in search of a clearer perspective on this existential question. His quest led him into the field of psychology, where he began to more tightly focus his inquiry and research on where, in everyday life, humans experience real happiness—the type of rich and soul-filling happiness that makes life worth living.

He focused his early research on creatives like musicians and artists who dedicated their lives to their craft despite, in many cases, having no expectation that their creativity would result in fame or fortune. They were, he surmised, among the purer examples of "following your passion." If it wasn't money or stardom, what made these creative pursuits worth their time and energy?

He learned that it was "that moment" they were all looking for—the same blissful and transfixed feeling I described above. As one of Mike's musician subjects explained, "You are in an ecstatic state to such a point that you feel as though you almost don't exist. I have experienced this time and again. My hand seems devoid of myself, and I have nothing to do with what is happening. I just sit there watching it in a state of awe and wonderment. And the music just flows out of itself."

But as he reflected on his own life, Mike realized that this feeling of exuberance and immersion that musicians describe feeling when in this state can happen outside of the creative realm. As an avid rock climber, Mike felt a very similar sensation as he doggedly scaled a difficult rock face. He was focused, energized, and totally engrossed in the climb.

Mike had an epiphany much like Martin Seligman had. As he became more fascinated with moments when people experienced true invigoration, Mike came to wonder: Why had the discipline of psychology focused almost entirely on studying human dysfunction? Why wasn't psychology equally focused on helping people *thrive*? Couldn't everything we know about human psychology be used to help humans find more of the best things in life, in addition to repairing the worst? How could he help people seek out the moments that bring a profound sense of enjoyment, or *flow*?

When we are in flow, not only do we experience a great sense of personal delight, but our performance goes through the roof.

Another researcher and flow junkie, Steven Kotler, describes this flow state as, "those moments of rapt attention and total absorption, when you get so focused on the task at hand that everything else disappears. Action and awareness merge. Your sense of self vanishes. Your sense of time distorts (either, typically, speeds up; or, occasionally, slows down)."[19]

Beyond creative pursuits, flow is also easily observed in athletic pursuits, likely because sports provide such a visible and calculable display of the flow state. It is easy to notice when someone is "totally in the zone" when every basketball shot they take is a score, or they're batting 1.000 in the past handful of baseball plate appearances.

In 1935, twenty-one-year-old runner Jesse Owens' flow state ushered in what has been dubbed "The Greatest Forty-Five Minutes in Sports." He set three track-and-field world records in just forty-five minutes at the Big Ten championships that year.

It happened again at the 1976 Olympic Games, when Romanian gymnast Nadia Comaneci executed her now-famous floor routine. The gymnast flawlessly nailed some of the most difficult stunts in the sport, earning her the first perfect ten ever awarded—one of seven she would achieve throughout the Games.

Perhaps most famously, it happened again during Michael Jordan's unstoppable performance in Game 1 of the 1992 NBA Finals between the Chicago Bulls and Portland Trail Blazers. He dropped six three-pointers in the first half alone, tying the Finals record at the time for three-pointers in a half. The game became

---

[19] Steven Kotler, "Frequently Asked Questions on Flow," accessed July 10, 2020, https://www.stevenkotler.com/rabbithole/ea-ullam-copy.

known as the "shrug game" for the now-legendary footage of Jordan looking over to the scorers table after his sixth triple of the night, shaking his head in disbelief, and shrugging as if to say, "Yeah, I can't believe these shots are falling either!"

When we are in flow, not only do we experience a great sense of personal delight, but our performance goes through the roof. Physically, our bodies move effortlessly. Our three-point shots seem to keep landing on nothing but net. Mentally, we are highly concentrated, creative, and able to draw on our greatest talents. Our brain feels clear and frictionless, like a freshly tuned, well-oiled engine, and we are able to sustain this focus for longer periods than normal, which improves our ability to tackle tough challenges or achieve big goals. Emotionally, our experience can be deeply fulfilling and feel intrinsically rewarding.

In these moments, our brain chemistry actually changes to enable these effects, serving up a powerful and performance-enhancing cocktail of chemicals that makes us sharper, faster, stronger, energized, and positive. Norepinephrine and dopamine team up to help us stay focused. Endorphins mitigate the effects of stress, and make the experience feel pleasurable. Anandamide inhibits fear, improves our thinking, and promotes greater creativity and risk-taking.

Achieving flow is like taking a speedball of potent, naturally occuring performance-enhancing drugs that work together to power this next-level state of consciousness. And it is important that our neurochemistry gives us this boost, as the types of activity that tend to lend themselves to achieving flow are commonly challenging ones, oftentimes stretching us outside of our perceived zone of competence and comfort.

MICHAEL JORDAN, CPA

You don't have to be Michael Jordan or an Olympic gymnast to find your flow state and tap into your brain's secret weapon. Although it is especially visible in athletics and music, flow can just as readily happen in the workplace.

I recall moments of flow during my analyst days when I found myself lost in building a financial model, only to look at the clock and realize I'd unknowingly been working at it into the wee hours of the morning. I was totally absorbed in the challenge. Everything else—including my concept of time and my appetite—simply fell away. The can of Red Bull that I had grabbed before I started sat there patiently, unopened on the side of my desk. I was dialed-in, operating on man-made energy of an entirely different sort.

For me, these invigorating experiences of flow come up again and again in brainstorming sessions, one-on-one meetings, and other business contexts. They have taught me that, fundamentally, we are all considerably more effective when our work involves activities that we find invigorating.

Neuroscience has an explanation for this. When we find and engage in activities that stimulate us in this way, the brain's wave activity calms to a steady alpha wave, which is smooth and free-flowing. In this alpha state, the noise generated by relentless neural firing that happens in our natural brain state weakens, creating the space for fewer and deeper neural connections. This shift from hyperactivity to hypoactivity dramatically enhances our focus and concentration and can help engender that feeling of effortlessness.

When we find flow, our prefrontal cortex—the more deliberative and sequential logic center of the brain—creates room for parallel processing in the more creative limbic regions of the brain, which sparks new, fresh, and spontaneous ways of thinking.

These effects combine to help us get better results—and faster—when we're flowing. It is no surprise that researchers credit flow with some of the most blockbuster scientific breakthroughs, some of the most astonishing athletic performances, some of the most inspiring guitar solos, and some of the greatest innovations of our time.

And it is a classic win-win—our companies get way more impact out of us, and we enjoy the process way more.

The idea of helping your team to identify and lean into their passions, and creating the conditions that allow them to flow in these activities, can be a real turbocharger for your company's success. The research tells us that we are considerably more effective when we are operating in this state; however, a study by McKinsey & Company concluded that most people spend only about 5 percent of their working hours here[20]. That means during thirty-eight hours out of every forty-hour work week, we are "under-optimized," functioning at a considerably lower level of effectiveness than we could be.

---

[20] Thomas Curran and Andrew P. Hill, "Perfectionism Is Increasing, and That's Not Good News," *Harvard Business Review*, January 26, 2018, https://hbr.org/2018/01/perfectionism-is-increasing-and-thats-not-good-news.

For most of the average person's working hours, it is like our car is stuck in first gear, expending a ton of energy, but moving at a low velocity.

What more is possible if we can help our teams find their fifth gear through activities that invigorate them and allow them to flow?

Stefan Falk is an executive performance and development coach whose work with leaders and organizations is heavily influenced by Csikszentmihalyi's flow theory. Falk latched onto Csikszentmihalyi's concept of "optimal challenge"—the idea that we are most likely to enter a flow state when we embrace a challenge that is stretchy, but still within our abilities and aligned with our talents. It is this same idea that has been a major driver of our team's success at my company, Alpine Investors. The founder has built the firm around taking high-potential professionals who are early in their career, handing them loads of responsibility that may initially exceed their experience level, and giving them leash but with a clear lifeline and lots of support. Then, we watch them rise to the challenge.

What we've learned is that the stretchier the challenge, the more successful people tend to be, and the neuroscience behind the flow state helps to explain why.

During thirty-eight hours out of every forty-hour work week, we are "under-optimized."

In his consulting work, Falk developed his own concept of "accelerated development," at the heart of which is the ability to form a clear mental picture of a long-term goal and attach good feelings to the imagined achievement of the goal. There is a boatload of research on the performance-enhancing benefits of this type of visualization. If you have well-defined goals—ones that you can visualize clearly—and regular feedback, you are more likely to get into a flow state.

Within my passion for music, this visualizing part is easy. One of my long-term-goals was to play guitar like Eric Clapton—a very stretchy goal, to be sure. Thanks to YouTube, I have a clear mental picture of how that looks and, believe me, there are delightful feelings when I visualize shredding it like the almighty Clapton! For the young Nadia Comaneci, it would have been to envision scoring perfect tens at the Olympic Games. For Michael Jordan, it would involve envisioning a rainstorm of three-pointers in one of those "can't miss" performances.

Falk took this wisdom to Swedish-owned multinational telecommunications company Ericsson, where he was faced with the classic business school case-study-esque task of merging two large business units, looking for rationalizations, and finding opportunities to increase productivity. In need of as much tailwind as he could create, Falk quickly introduced key elements of flow theory to his teams in the hopes it would fire up people's creative energies and drive greater performance to tackle the challenging task at hand.

Falk ensured that everyone at Ericsson could clearly envision what the long-term goal was—and how sweet it would taste when they got there. He made certain each had well-defined objectives and received high-quality feedback. He changed the practice of annual performance appraisals and introduced, instead, a bimonthly system of intensive ninety-minute one-on-one sessions in which managers would explore their teams' level of engagement with their challenges, and he ensured that he aligned each person with the types of activities in the workplan that most played to their passions—the ones in which they were most likely to feel invigorated and find flow.

The results were so impressive that Ericsson rolled out the system to all of their business units around the globe.

Riding high on the success at Ericsson, Falk moved on to the giant Swedish logistics and shipping organization Green Cargo. Drawing on the proof points from Ericsson, he devised a training program to introduce employees to the core concepts of flow and introduced regular monthly sessions with their managers, designed to assess whether everyone was facing the optimal level of challenge. Goals and assignments were adjusted as a result to encourage flow states in people's work.

In short order, the state-owned Green Cargo went on to turn a profit for the first time in its 120-year history, a result that executives ascribe directly to Falk's "flowcentric" program.

The corporate transformations Falk championed using the tenets of flow are valued at more than $2 billion.[21]

If leaders put people in a position where they are able to do what they are most passionate about, our businesses get the benefit of the surge in performance, and profit tends to follow.

---

[21] Stefan Falk, StefanFalk.net, accessed July 10, 2020, https://www.stefanfalk.net/.

ACTIONABLE: A STROLL DOWN MEMORY LANE

We learned earlier that many people struggle to find their passions. So how do we help them? Here's a good (and rather obvious) place to start: *think back to those that have left you invigorated before.*

What are the things in your life that have given you a real buzz while you were doing them?

Stop for a moment, and create a mental highlight reel of peak moments in your professional and personal life.

Start by rewinding the tape back to some of your earliest memories, through grade school and then high school, early adulthood, and so on. Put a mental pin in moments when you felt especially alive, those that had a particularly exhilarating or stimulating quality to them.

These were the moments in your life's journey when you were completely in the flow, when time seemed to fly by. When you seemed to be operating at a much higher level than normal. When you felt fully alive, resonating with the world around you like the vibration of a tuning fork when it strikes a strong, clear note. As you pass these moments on your stroll down memory lane, stop at a few, and ask yourself:

- *Who (if anyone) were you with?*
- *What were you doing?*
- *Who were you being?*
- *What adjectives would you use to describe how it felt in that moment?*

Pay particular attention to the activities that most drew you in before age ten, before the temptations of money, prestige, and affirmation clouded your view. It is in this early chapter of life that we find the purest form of what invigorates us. As is the case with music and creativity for me, the things that brought us joy when we were ten are oftentimes still things that bring us joy now.

(Tempting as it may be to read on, pause here. Reread the exercise above and go for it. Really do it. I promise, it will be worth it.)

Now, pick a few of those moments and dig a layer deeper beneath the surface of the moment itself. What was it about the activity that you were engaged in that so enlivened you?

Let me help you understand what I mean by going back to the personal example of playing music. Sure, the act of playing music itself is rewarding—it is challenging, collaborative, and active. And its product—(hopefully) pretty music—is pleasing. But when I dig to the root of what enlivens me about playing music, it is two things:

The opportunity to create something from nothing.
And the opportunity to collaborate—and connect—with others in doing that.

Understanding, at the most fundamental level, what made these activities so invigorating is key. It then allows me to seek out other activities that can play to those same intrinsic motivations.

You'll likely see dots starting to connect across some of the peak moments you have experienced. Themes that link together why, at a deeper level, certain activities feel so exhilarating and enriching to you.

We are considerably more effective when we are motivated primarily by the fun, excitement, and enjoyment of an activity.

When I stop to think about it, it turns out, this idea of enjoying "the opportunity to create something from nothing" characterizes a good handful of the things in life that bring me the most energy. It is a large part of what had me wonderfully lost in building a financial model into the wee hours of the morning during my early career. Nothing existed at the beginning—just a blank spreadsheet. And, brick by brick, a magnificent and nerdy palace of financial insight was built.

And knowing that activities with this characteristic are highly intrinsically rewarding to me can help me to actively seek out more chances to put this passion to work—at my job, at home, in my community, and so on.

As you start to get in touch with the root motivations that tend to make certain activities enlivening to you, it can open up an exciting new field of possibilities.

Ask yourself: *what are all of the different activities—both on my current professional path and beyond—that can allow me to do what invigorates me?*

TARGET ACTIVITIES THAT YOU FIND INTRINSICALLY MOTIVATING

What activities are you naturally motivated to do? What are you most willing to put effort into?

A study by Harvard Business School professor Teresa Amabile showed that we are considerably more effective when we are motivated primarily by the fun, excitement, and enjoyment of an activity than when our motivation is centered around extrinsic forces like awards, money, or fame.

As part of a study, Amabile brought twenty-three artists together for an art show. Each one brought ten pieces of commissioned art (created at the specific direction of a commercial buyer) and ten pieces of noncommissioned art (created by the artist for their own enjoyment or expression). The commissioned and noncommissioned works were interspersed and arranged randomly for a group of art critics to peruse and rate.

It turns out, the art that had been created on commission was, on average, rated as *significantly* less creative than the works of art that were noncommissioned.[22]

Daniel Pink, who referenced this study in his bestseller *Drive*, made an important point when it comes to how these learnings map to the workplace. "[The study shows that] artists do their best work in noncommissioned conditions, yet we have a problem because if we go to our workplaces throughout North America, there's almost no 'noncommissioned work.' "

In other words, workers often don't have the liberty to work on things that play to their deepest intrinsic motivations.

Instead, as leaders, we often mistakenly rely too heavily on extrinsic motivators like money, promotions, and the like to attempt to stimulate performance. Overrelying on these can undercut the more potent intrinsic motivators, something known as the "Overjustification Effect."

A meta-analysis by researcher Tim Judge, which reviewed findings from over ninety studies on the motivational effects of money, found that beyond a certain

---

[22] Teresa Amabile, "How to Kill Creativity." In Steven Johnson (Ed.), The Innovator's Cookbook: Essentials for Inventing What Is Next (New York: Riverhead Books, 2011), pp. 38–63.

level of income that allows for basic needs to be met, the relationship between money and job satisfaction is very weak—and it holds across cultures and countries.[23] What's more, "for every standard deviation increase in [monetary] reward, intrinsic motivation for interesting tasks decreases by about 25 percent." This means that strategies that focus primarily on the use of extrinsic motivators run a serious risk of diminishing, rather than promoting, the types of intrinsic motivation that make us both more effective in our work and more fulfilled.

This is, in part, because these incentive schemes run the risk of keeping us focused on ourselves, at the expense of focusing on our contributions to others—which, as we will discuss in the next chapter, can create a deeper sense of meaning in the work that we're doing, and unlock greater discretionary effort.

It's true that the lure of extrinsic motivation—like money, prestige, and external validation—is all around us. Legendary venture capitalist Paul Graham, founder of Y Combinator, warns of the dangers of chasing external validation.

> "What you should not do, I think, is worry about the opinion of anyone beyond your friends. You shouldn't worry about prestige. Prestige is the opinion of the rest of the world. Prestige is like a powerful magnet that warps even your beliefs about what you enjoy. It causes you to work not on what you like, but what you'd like to like. Prestige is just fossilized inspiration. If you do anything well enough, you'll make it prestigious. Plenty of things we now consider prestigious were anything but at first. Jazz comes to mind—though almost any established art form would do. So just do what you like, and let prestige take care of itself."[24]

RECRAFT YOUR ROLE TO ALLOW FOR MORE OF THE INVIGORATING STUFF

"Great jobs can be made, not just found." — *Shane Lopez, Ph. D*

In order to get the most out of our people, we have to help them find ways to engage in the types of activities that tap into their deepest intrinsic motivations, ones that will make the work they do feel stimulating, enriching, and enlivening. We have to find opportunities for them to, metaphorically speaking, create beautiful pieces of noncommissioned art.

---

[23] Tomas Chamorro-Premuzic, "Does Money Really Affect Motivation? A Review of the Research," *Harvard Business Review*, April 10, 2013, https://hbr.org/2013/04/does-money-really-affect-motiv.
[24] Paul Graham, "How to Do What You Love," PaulGraham.com, January 2006, http://www.paulgraham.com/love.html.

The idea of "job crafting" has come to the fore in recent years, referring to the reformulation of our role and responsibilities to better align with our Blue Flame—what we can do best, what is intrinsically motivating for us, what we care about. When our job description is full of responsibilities and activities that we find invigorating, it is far likelier to produce our greatest contributions. Unsurprisingly, studies have shown that job crafting promotes greater engagement.[25]

Getting the immense benefits that job crafting can offer has four layers to it:

1. Knowing what lights your people up: Develop a clear understanding of what types of activities your teammates are most passionate about, and what activities they are each most talented at. The exercises and discussion guides in Chapter 11 can be very useful in helping you to architect a Blue Flame conversation that will help you to uncover these things.

2. Reformulating their role: Rejig responsibilities in a way that brings the role into alignment with the types of activities that are most energizing to your teammates, and into alignment with their greatest talents. This involves reconsidering the types, scope, and number of responsibilities that make up their job. As we discussed earlier, an important element of this is ensuring that the recrafted role is enjoyably challenging. It should feel stretchy ("This is going to be tough, but I know I can do it."), but not unachievable or stressful ("This is going to be tough; and I don't think I have the talents, resources, or motivation to be successful.").

3. Connecting the dots: Understand clearly the connection between what lights your employees up and the newly reengineered role. And keep that connection alive. Your employee needs to internalize the connection so that it remains clear to them in the heat of battle that the work they are doing ought to strike the type of chord that has them skipping into the office. And you, as their leader, have a responsibility to constantly draw attention to how the role they are in plays to their greatest intrinsic motivations.

4. Creating the conditions: Help your teammates to find flow in the work they are doing. Csikszentmihalyi's research offers a handful of tips on how to create a set of conditions that can help trigger flow. Things like helping your employees

---

[25] Catherine Moore, "What Is Job Crafting? (Incl. 5 Examples and Exercises)," PositivePsychology.com, June 8, 2020, https://positivepsychology.com/job-crafting/.

develop a clear and exciting vision of the goal, and what the reward will feel like when they achieve it. And ensuring that the goal is "stretchy"—giving them just enough challenge to keep them totally engrossed and firing on all cylinders, but not being so challenging that it outstrips their capabilities.

Here's an example of how these four steps look in action.

I held a leadership role in an education business and got to know our curriculum expert, Stephanie. A former educator herself, she was totally plugged into all aspects of the K–12 education system, which equipped her well to support the product development and marketing teams from behind the scenes.

She would send around vital updates on developments to the various curricula that affected our products, and she really enjoyed working with product managers and marketing copywriters to help devise up-to-the-minute product enhancements and compelling marketing copy. Stephanie was enjoying her job—kinda. In a one-on-one Blue Flame conversation with her, it became clear that while she loved the mission and enjoyed the subject matter of her work, she felt she was under-contributing.

"What do you feel is missing from your current role?" I asked.

She hesitated for a moment, but was soon able to answer.

"I feel I'm sending out stuff that only those that 'need to know' may ever read, but understanding what is going on in the classroom is actually at the heart of nearly *everything* that we do. See, Dan, things are evolving quickly in education right now, and our teams—from product, to marketing, to sales, to operations—need to be totally plugged in to what is happening in the market. Not to mention, of course, our executive team … who run the risk of getting too far removed from what's going on in the everyday lives of our customers."

She paused.

"So I guess I feel I could contribute a lot more, which would benefit the company, and would get me more engaged. I guess when it comes down to it, I *love* teaching people things. This is why I got into education in the first place! And if I can make arithmetic exciting to fourth graders, I can make this stuff interesting to our teams!"

This was one of the easier Blue Flame conversations. Stephanie was clear on what she can do best, what invigorates her, and what brings her meaning. All I had to do was encourage Stephanie to lean harder into the types of activities that she finds really stimulating, and find ways that those can have a bigger impact on the business.

Stephanie jumped in headfirst.

She approached our HR team about doing a special onboarding training for all new employees, which she titled "What's Happening in Our Customers' Lives." HR jumped in headfirst, too! She started offering regular lunch-and-learn sessions for anyone who wanted to attend. She even plucked up the courage to approach senior management, and her briefings are now a regular item in executive team meetings.

It was obvious to everyone what Stephanie had to offer. She knows our educational system in detail and in depth. She is passionate about it. The opportunity to better equip our business teams to create things that can enrich the lives of students and teachers is meaningful to her, and brought a deeper sense of purpose to her role. And she is uniquely qualified to teach this stuff.

Stephanie was able to reformulate her role, expand its scope and responsibilities, and reshape it from one that was largely behind-the-scenes to one that was actively serving and equipping the most critical market-facing business teams. Across the board, the company became much more plugged into the realities of what was happening in the classroom, and in our customers' lives—a most crucial input to our overall business strategy. The business and our customers benefited big-time.

Stephanie's is a simple story that not only shows the impact of Blue Flames on the workplace, but also how integral it is for leadership to help people reimagine their roles in a way that can bring them close to it.

But let's be real about the fact that it is nearly impossible to job-craft away all of the less exciting stuff from someone's job description. What about the inevitable responsibilities of one's job that don't register highly on their passion-meter? After all, someone has to take out the trash and fill out the TPS reports. Even Stephanie can't spend every moment of her day flowing around the office.

In this way, "follow your passion" is idealistic, and can possibly set unrealistically high expectations about the level of bliss we can be expected to feel at every moment of every day. Even Stephanie will still encounter tasks and projects that will feel considerably less stimulating, even a drag.

But if you are able to spend substantial time in your work life doing things that you are passionate about, you'll find the inevitable grind worth grinding for.

FIND THE DELIGHT IN WHAT YOU ALREADY DO

"I never once hated this job. I fell in love with my work and gave my life to it. Even though I'm eighty-five years old, I don't feel like retiring." — *Jiro Ono*

Buried beneath the glamorous shopping arcades of Ginza district in Tokyo's Chuo City, a tiny and unassuming ten-seat restaurant sits in the basement of an office block and faces a subway platform of the city's Metro transit system. The fact that there is a sushi bar there is not surprising, as there are over three thousand in Tokyo alone. But the fact that Barack Obama was entertained there by Japan's prime minister Shinzo Abe in 2014 and that the restaurant has been awarded three Michelin stars every year since 2007 (when the prestigious restaurant guide first launched its Tokyo edition) makes this particular sushi restaurant a bit more noteworthy than most.

The restaurant, Sukiyabashi Jiro, is run by its sushi chef owner, Jiro Ono. Ono ran away from home at the age of nine and took up an apprenticeship in a sushi restaurant. Now in his nineties, Ono has been preparing and serving sushi ever since.

Sukiyabashi Jiro recently lost its three Michelin stars—not because the quality of the sushi has slipped, but because the restaurant has become so exclusive that it is no longer possible for the general public to book a table. Evidently, being Prime Minister of Japan seems to help.

Diners are asked not to be late, as the rice is cooked to perfection to coincide with their precise arrival time. Women are also asked not to wear strong perfume because the scent will disturb the flavor of the twenty exquisitely prepared sushi pieces that form the fixed menu of the day, which varies with the seasons. If your appetite is not hearty enough to manage all twenty courses, the chefs will adjust your portion size. The recommended beverage is green tea, which refreshes the palate.

After a heart attack at the age of seventy—more than twenty years ago—Ono gave up smoking and also stopped his daily bicycle ride to Tokyo's famous Tsukiji fish market to select the fish for the day's menu. His elder son, who will take over the restaurant when Ono someday hangs up his apron, now makes the daily trip. His son is also a master, a designation that required him to first apprentice for ten years with Ono.

If you are able to spend substantial time in your work life doing things that you are passionate about, you'll find the inevitable grind worth grinding for.

Like a true craftsman, Ono constantly experiments with new sushi pieces, striving for perfection. To this day, as he stands behind the serving counter and watches his customers eat their meticulously served sushi selection, he notes their reactions and uses that firsthand customer intel to further hone his craft. He does this all at the age of ninety-four, an age at which many in the world are long retired.

Ono, a committed and contented artisan, is extraordinarily happy with the work that he does. It is clear that it is the type of "happy" that sits deep within his bones—a sort of bliss. Like the residents of Okinawa whom we introduced you to in Chapter 2, Ono has found joy in—not to mention a world-class talent for—his work that keeps him vital in his old age.

Ono offers a unique perspective on finding what invigorates you. "Once you decide on your occupation," says Ono, "you must immerse yourself in your work. *You have to fall in love with your work.*"

At first glance, his perspective may seem self-evident: "Yeah, do what you love, or love what you do. Got it." However, there is an important distinction from the often-peddled advice to "follow your passion." Ono's wisdom, by contrast, is to *love the work we have chosen*. This requires that we consciously cultivate love for and delight in the work that we are doing.

This highlights a limitation in the "follow your passion" way of thinking. It implies you either have passion for something, or you don't. And you must search to find it until you have landed on that role, career, or vocation that perfectly awakens it.

Sure, there are activities that are fundamentally more enriching based on what you find enjoyable, and based in part on where your greatest talents lie. And make no mistake, this book is a call to action to encourage and support leaders in helping their people discover what lights them up and orient their careers and lives accordingly. But this assumption that passion is singular and unchanging can deprive us of a chance to find it in new places, and to cultivate passion for activities and responsibilities that are already in our flight path.

Professor Jon Jachimowicz warns us of this pitfall:

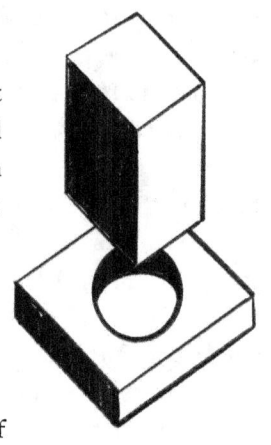

"We may try many different jobs looking for the right 'fit,' the role that instantly flips the passion switch, and we may not take into account the fact that it often takes time to develop one's passion for a job, along with the skills, confidence, and relationships that allow one to experience passion for work. Indeed, research has shown that believing passion is fixed can make people less likely to explore new topics—potential new sources of passion. It also leads people to give up on new pursuits more quickly if they seem difficult."[26]

But this idea of the "right fit" is just as much a mindset as it is dependent on the actual job. Our experience of the world is shaped by our attitude and belief toward it—and in the same way, our experience of our work is shaped by our belief toward it.

Although we may not always have control of the experiences themselves, we have ample control over how we experience the experiences. In other words, whether something is highly invigorating or a total drag is a matter of our perspective toward it, and our perspectives are malleable.

Let's take an everyday example. You are heading to a weekly departmental report-out meeting at the office, and you're totally dreading it. Viscerally. *These meetings tend to be as boring as watching paint dry*, you tell yourself, *chock-full of mundane status updates on things in other departments that aren't even relevant to my job. Can I get back to my real work now?*

---

[26] Jon M. Jachimowicz, "3 Reasons It's So Hard to 'Follow Your Passion,' " *Harvard Business Review*, October 15, 2019, https://hbr.org/2019/10/3-reasons-its-so-hard-to-follow-your-passion.

Here, you are stuck in one perspective: that this meeting will definitively and inarguably be a real snoozer. But when we're caught up in our loathing, we fail to see alternative perspectives.

Alternative perspectives like, "Gee, this is a really cool opportunity for me to learn about what's going on in other parts of the company, which can help me see how all of the different gears of the machine fit together! I'll bet that being exposed to what these other teams are up against can help me find new ways that my team can help them out."

Or, "It feels like these ho-hum meetings, which could be so much more than just report-outs, present a great opportunity for me to do what I love, which is listen intently and surface new creative ideas about the challenges and opportunities that each group is facing. That could be fun for me and beneficial to the group."

Which one of these will make the meeting the most enriching and productive? Which is going to maximize your impact in these meetings?

The meeting is happening no matter what you do. Instead of griping about it, let alone quitting to find the perfect job that doesn't subject you to these lame meetings, choose a more empowering perspective.

We talked about flowmaster Stefan Falk a little earlier. Here is a quote from one of his clients that is especially relevant here:

> "I know that when I view a task as boring my mind starts to work slower as well as tend to wander and think of other things I'd rather be doing, which means that I will perform the task even worse. Hence, this will make the task extraordinarily boring! Over time I have learnt that there are virtually no boring tasks, *only boring ways to think about tasks*. This way of thinking is now part of my intrinsic thought pattern so I automatically—and with no additional effort—manage to identify all exciting aspects of the tasks I am facing. I realize that this aspect of my developed character is one of my core assets." [27]

---

[27] Stefan Falk, "The Traits of Distinctive People," StefanFalk.net, July 5, 2013, https://www.stefanfalk.net/uploads/5/4/1/1/54112761/white_paper_the_traits_of_distinctive_people_web.pdf.

ACTIONABLE: UNLOCK DELIGHT

We can help ourselves, and our people, to find the delight in what we are already doing with these unlocking questions:

- *What is it about the work that you do that is delightful? What can you revel in?*
- *What have been moments of pure joy that you have experienced in the work that you do?*
- *When you stop to think about it, what is extraordinary about even the ordinary moments in your role?*
- *What can you do today to increase your positive impact on your team and your company?*

IN CASE YOU MISSED IT: THE KEY IDEAS

They Call Me Flow: Mike Csikszentmihalyi coined and popularized the term "flow" to describe the state of pure absorption and enjoyment that we experience when we are doing activities that we are passionate about.

Everybody Wins: When we are doing activities that we find invigorating, we tend to get better results, faster. Our brain chemistry actually changes in a way that can make us sharper, faster, stronger, energized, and more positive. Finding this flow state is one of those classic win-wins—our companies get way more impact out of us, and we enjoy the process way more.

The Edge Your Team Needs: What would be possible if we could help our teams find a new gear through their passions? And how can we do this? There are a few ways:

- *Invite your team to take a stroll down memory lane.* What have been the things in their life that have given them a real buzz while they were doing them? What was it about those moments that made them feel so stimulated? Who were they with? What were they doing? And what are all of different activities—both on their current professional path and beyond—that can allow them to do more of what they find invigorating?

- *Help them to home in on activities that they find intrinsically motivating.* We are considerably more effective when we are motivated primarily by the fun, excitement, and enjoyment of an activity than when our motivation is centered around extrinsic forces like awards, money, or fame.

- *Support them in recrafting their role to allow them to do more of the invigorating stuff.* This involves the reformulation of one's role and responsibilities to better align with what is most intrinsically motivating for them, which we know is likelier to produce their greatest contributions.

- *Help them find delight in the work they already do.* To "love the work that they have chosen." Help them discover the things that they can find delight in when it comes to the work they are already doing.

PART 04

Purpose: Do What You Care Deeply About

CHAPTER 9

What Do You Care Deeply About?

Helping your team to discover their Blue Flame extends beyond identifying activities that they find to be *invigorating*. It is also about helping them to discover and invest themselves in things they care deeply about—things that create in them a sense of *purpose*. Doing so gives their work a sense of meaning. A stake. A cause. A raison d'être. It gives it soul. It can transform a career into a calling.

Without purpose of this sort, our work can feel like constantly pushing a boulder up a hill, only to watch it roll down after great effort and toil. At worst, life and work can feel hollow, or rotten inside.

★ ★ ★

Scott Harrison spent his early adult life making a great deal of money and spending a considerable portion of it on a viciously indulgent, self-centered lifestyle. After an epiphany that caused him to confront the fact that he was "emotionally and spiritually bankrupt"—his Blue Flame completely unlit—he left it all behind in search of a life and career that was far more meaningful. The impact on his life, and on the world, has been extraordinary.

Harrison was raised in a conservative Christian household. He spent much of his childhood caring for his mother, whose immune system was damaged by carbon monoxide poisoning caused by a faulty gas boiler in their home. She would have a severe allergic reaction to almost any chemical—including ink on the pages of books. She spent most of her time on a bed in a bathroom breathing through a charcoal-filter mask. Harrison and his father used to bake books in the oven to drive off the more volatile chemicals and Harrison would take the books to his mother inside cellophane bags, which she would handle with gloves.

At the age of eighteen, in somewhat of a rebellious move following his difficult childhood, Harrison set off for New York City with his band, which broke up shortly after.

Harrison discovered that his talents and passions lent themselves to creating musical events, which kept him close to the same passion for music that had drawn him to New York in the first place. He organized New York City's first R&B Open Mic night and went on to build a successful business by, as he puts it, "creating an environment, a culture, where artists would want to come and try out material. A safe space." Famous artists did come: people like Stevie Wonder, Brian McKnight, Prince, and Whitney Houston.

Then someone challenged Harrison to replicate the same idea in the fashion arena, which he took as a dare. Drawing on the same talents of persuasiveness and relationship-building, he hit the phones. He finally persuaded one club to give him their quietest night of the week, and hit the phones again to drum up interest in the fashion showcase he was envisioning. It worked. Over time, he promoted fashion events at over thirty nightclubs.

Business was good. "All you had to do was get the most beautiful people inside the right nightclub," says Harrison, "and if you did that you could charge the most astronomical amounts for liquor."

Then—by Harrison's own admission—his life began to veer off course.

Drinks companies started to pay Harrison and his partner monthly retainers simply for them to be seen drinking certain brands of booze at their table at nightclub events. Spending most of his working days drunk in nightclubs didn't do much for Harrison's mental health. After some years of this lifestyle, Harrison developed a coughing problem—caused by the two packs of Marlboro he smoked each day, a serious drinking problem, a drug problem ("everything short of heroin"), and a gambling problem.

At an event in an opulent compound in South America where Dom Perignon was being served by the gallon, Harrison hit a breaking point, which led to an important realization. He suddenly understood that even though he supposedly had everything he could want—a New York City apartment, an expensive car, a model girlfriend—he was "the most deeply unhappy person I knew." He describes himself as spiritually and emotionally bankrupt and "just rotted" inside. He decided he wanted a life that was the exact opposite of his current life.

He longed for, in a word, *meaning*.

Activated by this realization, Harrison sold everything he owned and gave up cigarettes, alcohol, and drugs overnight. He went to work as a photojournalist on a Mercy Ship—an NGO that supplies hospital ships—off the coast of Liberia, a country that had just emerged from a bitter civil war that had killed around a quarter of a million people. Photojournalism in Liberia wasn't a calling that Harrison sought out, but when the opportunity came up, he seized it as a chance to do something radically different. The hope was that it would help foster a radical shift in his life.

Like all of the crew members and doctors on board the Mercy Ship, Harrison not only gave his service for free, he paid "crew fees" to help cover the costs of his bed and board. While he had discovered that making money did not make him happy, the experience helped him realize that being of service *did* make him happy.

The volunteer doctors and surgeons from the ship set up temporary onshore hospitals and put up posters inviting people to visit. Thousands turned up looking for treatment for a huge range of conditions: cataracts, war wounds, burns, cleft palates, broken limbs, and disfiguring facial tumors.

Harrison took tens of thousands of photographs of the ship's doctors at work. He sent some of his photographs to his 15,000-strong "club list"—the beautiful partygoers he used to invite to his nightclub events. Some, perhaps unsurprisingly, quickly unsubscribed, but Harrison was struck by the number who asked how they could help. They offered money, and some even offered to join the ship and help in any way they could.

It dawned on Harrison that he could use the very same talents he had employed to build his nightclub business—his tenacity, his persuasiveness, his ability to paint a compelling picture of something that didn't yet exist, and his organizational skills—as a force for good. In his own words, he realized he could use his talents "to redeem the thing [he] did for ten years and [create] a different story; to promote something completely different, something that actually mattered."

He went back to New York and set up a photographic exhibition and gala fundraiser, displaying his photographs and sharing details of the ship's work in Liberia. The event raised $100,000 for the charity. He returned to the hospital ship to work for a second year.

The ship's latest work included a range of community development projects, including AIDS education, maternity and dental clinics, and water sanitation. It was during this tour of duty that Harrison first saw people drinking water from what he describes as "swamps"—muddy ponds that were the only source of water for whole communities. He learned that over 50 percent of Liberians had no access to clean water. He couldn't help but think back to the days when water at his events would be sold for $10 a bottle, and would often stay unopened on the table as the crowd indulged in $500 bottles of champagne instead.

Then and there, Harrison made it his mission in life to play his part in helping to ensure that clean water is available to everyone on the planet. He cast a vision—which still fuels him today—of a world where no human being would be without access to clean water just because of where they were born.

In 2006, he launched Charity: Water. The charity's operating costs are funded by private donors, so that 100 percent of donations from the public can be spent on their projects. The charity is "solution agnostic," working with thirty-seven different local partners to provide whatever solution best fits the local problem: hand-dug wells, deep-bore wells, rainwater harvesting, pipes bringing water from mountain springs, and filtration systems.

Harrison's organization currently has over 1 million supporters worldwide, and has sponsored over 51,000 water projects bringing clean water to over 11 million people in developing countries.[28,29,30]

In the same way that finding something that he cared deeply about catalyzed Harrison's impact on the world, helping our teammates find real meaning in what they do is yet another source of free fuel, one that many leaders and their teams are missing out on.

According to a BetterUp survey, only one in twenty respondents rated their current jobs as providing the most meaningful work they could imagine. Yet

---

[28] "Meet the Founder," Charity: Water, accessed July 10, 2020, https://www.charitywater.org/about/scott-harrison-story/.
[29] "Scott Harrison: The Secret Formula for Finding Your Passion," *Impact Theory*, October 9, 2018, https://impacttheory.com/episode/scott-harrison/.
[30] Scott Harrison, "New York City Art Exhibition and Gala Fundraiser," accessed July 10, 2020, http://www.onamercyship.com/2005/07/new-york-city-art-exhibition-and-gala.html.

for decades, Americans have ranked finding meaning in their work as their top priority when it comes to taking or staying with a job—above promotions, income, job security, and hours.[31]

Our people are yearning for purpose—to do work that is meaningful—but few are finding it.

What's more, nine out of ten employees polled by a group of researchers, led by bestselling author and psychologist Shawn Achor, indicated they would be willing to trade a percentage of their lifetime earnings for greater meaning at work. Across age and salary groups, workers want meaningful work badly enough that they're willing to pay for it. That's right, there is a world where your teammates are potentially paid less, but are more joyful about their work, and create much more profit for your company.

Studies show that when leaders manage to capture people's hearts (not just their heads) by helping them to find meaning in what they do, they will give us up to 40 percent more discretionary effort. These employees who care deeply about their work are on average 32 percent more committed to their jobs, have 46 percent higher job satisfaction, and perform 16 percent better than other employees.[32]

Fundamentally, humans long to feel meaning and significance in the work they do—and are able to be considerably more effective *and* fulfilled when they find it.

In his book *Man's Search for Meaning*, Viktor Frankl writes about his time in Nazi concentration camps—where his father, mother, and sister died—and the enlightenment and meaning he was able to find even in this horrific environment. Frankl lost everything during his imprisonment, but he was able to hold on to one thing it turns out nobody can take away: *"The last of the human freedoms: to choose one's attitude in any given set of circumstances, to choose one's own way."* Frankl asserts that we may not always be able to choose the situations we find ourselves in, but we can still choose our reaction and our perspective toward it. (Sound familiar from the last chapter?)

---

[31] Wayne F. Cascio, "Changes in Workers, Work, and Organizations," *Handbook of Psychology*, April 15, 2003, https://onlinelibrary.wiley.com/doi/abs/10.1002/0471264385.wei1216.

[32] Shawn Achor et al., "9 Out of 10 People Are Willing to Earn Less Money to Do More-Meaningful Work," *Harvard Business Review*, November 6, 2018, https://hbr.org/2018/11/9-out-of-10-people-are-willing-to-earn-less-money-to-do-more-meaningful-work.

The core of Frankl's belief, inspired by his life experience, was that life can have meaning even in the most challenging of circumstances. He posited that the truest motivation for living comes from finding that meaning: a reason for being.

This extends much deeper than finding activities that energize and invigorate you, an idea we covered in the last chapter. Think of passions as things that give us energy, while purpose is something that makes us feel a real sense of heart. While these are different, you will see that the two can become tightly interlaced as fuel for the Blue Flame.

Our thirst for finding purpose in the work we do arises from the inherent altruistic motivations that we have as humans. As a species, we evolved with a built-in propensity to take care of others. We are innately empathetic, despite the theories in Western culture that people are inherently selfish and cruel. This idea that humans are a self-interested bunch was promoted by the philosopher Thomas Hobbes in his book *Leviathan*, and reinforced some time later by author Ayn Rand, whose fiction writing cast a bright light on human self-centeredness. Look no further than movies like *The Wolf of Wall Street* to get a modern-day taste of the same worldview. Or most political news outlets ... but we won't go there.

No doubt, the wars, crimes, and injustices that litter news headlines, and strike close to home for each of us in different ways, paint a mixed picture of human motivation. Case in point: in 2013, two humans pressed the detonator button on homemade pressure cooker bombs at the finish line of the Boston Marathon, killing three people and leaving dozens gravely injured. But seconds later on that very same day, other humans were seen running into harm's way to help save the wounded, sacrificing their own lives in doing so.

It is clearly myopic to label humans either as categorically egocentric or altruistic.

Our people are yearning for purpose—to do work that is meaningful—but few are finding it.

But human biology and social science give us hope that humans are built with hardwiring that creates a strong capacity for altruism. There are evolutionary and social reasons why humans have evolved in this way, but neuroscience gives us the clearest explanation on why humans behave selflessly: the reward centers in the brain are activated when we carry out an altruistic act. In short, we derive pleasure from helping others.

Evolutionarily, we probably ended up this way because serving the collective was critical to our survival in the old days. You might remember old Happy-Go-Lucky and his tribe of fellow cavemen, cavewomen, and cavebabies (plus the very few cavegrandmas and -grandpas who managed to survive into the Stone Age equivalent of "old age"). Because of his generally trustworthy, carefree disposition, Happy got gobbled up by an encroaching saber-toothed tiger, while his more paranoid buddies who grabbed a sharpened stick and chased the predator off survived. The vigilant survivors left their lineage with a genetic oversupply of the same negativity bias that helped keep them off the tiger's dinner menu.

Humans are built with hardwiring that creates a strong capacity for altruism.

In this same era, the tribe learned to rely on cooperative behaviors to improve their chances of survival. When they hunted and foraged, it worked better if they coordinated their actions. They were able to bag more food if they communicated their goals and strategies so that others could adapt and collaborate, as opposed to squabbling and fighting among themselves. Doing so allowed them to survive longer.

Then there was the question of a fair division of the spoils. How would they divide up the freshly hunted woolly mammoth steak and the gathered berries and roots? Maybe a young boy we'll call Why-Should-I-Help-Others hadn't pulled his weight in the hunt again and his fellow cavepeople weren't so sure he deserved his full share. And maybe the cavewomen were thinking that Why-Should-I-Help-Others wasn't the most reliable provider for their future cavebabies—plus no one liked him anyway. So every time he approached the caveladies at the cavebar, hoping for a chance to procreate, they turned an Ice Age cold shoulder. In this way, Why-Should-I-Help-Others' genes didn't last long in the gene pool, being pushed out by the more caring, helpful cavedudes.

Then there was the issue of childcare. The tribe's few remaining cavegrandmas weren't very productive anymore—but giving them their fair share of the available food and resources kept them alive to look after cavebabies while the cavemoms and cavedads hunted and foraged.

All of these "altruistic" behaviors gave the tribe an advantage over the other tribes competing for scarce resources in their area. It also gave them an advantage when it came to defending themselves against attacks by predators or other cavepeeps—you know, strength in numbers. Tribe members who were prepared to put themselves at risk to defend the tribe were hugely advantageous to the tribe's survival—and many of them would survive to pass on their selflessness genes to future generations.

David Sloan Wilson, professor of biology and anthropology at Binghamton University and the author of *Does Altruism Exist?*, argues that social science and biology agree: cooperative groups do better than less altruistic ones. Over the course of evolution, this began to suppress competition within groups, and encourage empathy. And thanks to the evolutionary law of survival of the fittest, supportive group behavior and generosity are now hardwired into our brains.

Throughout the ages since, great thinkers have understood the importance of altruism not only to human survival, but to self-actualization. They have consistently pointed us back to the same universal truth: the deepest sense of fulfillment humans can hope to achieve in life is often found by helping others.

As we discussed earlier, we are wired for negativity bias—to seek out and focus on the negative stuff. This is one of the reasons why news headlines are so skewed toward *what's wrong*—the heartbreak, injustice, and crime. But we aren't cavepeople anymore, and we can't let this outdated brain wiring cloud our ability to see the countless, everyday examples of selflessness.

Just today, I grabbed these from the news headlines:

"Alabama Man Who Mows Lawns for Elderly Now Delivers Free Meals"

"This Man Is a Veterinarian Who Walks Around California and Treats Homeless People's Animals for Free"

"87-Year-Old Woman Spent Months Knitting 75 Hats to Keep Strangers Warm This Winter"

" 'I Can, So I Will': Woman Shares Story of Giving Kidney to a Complete Stranger"

Few examples demonstrate how deeply our altruistic impulses can run than live organ and tissue donations—living donors giving a kidney, bone marrow, blood, liver tissue, etc., to an unknown recipient in need.

My brother Michael was an active and seemingly healthy twenty-five-year-old when he got the bad news. After weeks of gradually increasing fatigue and a battery of tests, Michael was diagnosed with acute lymphocytic leukemia (ALL), a rapidly advancing form of blood and bone marrow cancer that usually afflicts people much older than him. Naturally, our family was stunned—but both fortunately and unfortunately, I suppose, this wasn't our first rodeo given my brother Jonny's bout with and triumph over pediatric cancer years earlier.

The intervention for ALL that most improves the chances of long-term survival is a bone marrow transplant, although this requires that a match be available. Doctors first sought a match within the family, which each of our siblings was eagerly tested for. But unfortunately, no dice. So, doctors began searching the national bone marrow donor registry, which at the time was considerably less extensive than it is now. After several months of nerve-wracking waiting, during which Michael was fighting for his life through grueling chemotherapy treatments, he got the call: the doctors believed they had found a match.

His donor, whom we will call Jane, lived just forty-five minutes from Michael in Ohio, a lucky and perhaps divinely inspired coincidence. Jane was a salt-of-the-earth, fifty-something woman who had children about Michael's age. She entered the national bone marrow registry on a whim in the early 2000s, perhaps not expecting she would ever get the call. But when she did, it was, in her words, a "real no-brainer decision."

Relative to other forms of organ and tissue donation, bone marrow donation is less invasive with lesser pain and lower risk of complication. Nonetheless, as a result of the drugs that donors take leading up to the extraction procedure, they may experience flu-like symptoms—headache, bone pain, muscle aches—for several days prior to the collection, as well as mild-to-moderate symptoms following the treatment. A small portion of donors experience more severe complications. The question you're probably asking is: *Why would a person endure any level of pain and personal risk in service to a complete stranger?*

As you might expect, it turns out that altruism—giving of ourselves in service to another—is deeply personally gratifying to the donors.[33] In fact, studies have shown that those who choose to be organ donors have turned out to have a bit of extra material in the region of the brain that produces empathy.

---

[33] E. K. Massey et al., "Encouraging Psychological Outcomes After Altruistic Donation to a Stranger," *American Journal of Transplantation*, Volume 10, Issue 6, June 2010, pages 1445-1452, https://onlinelibrary.wiley.com/doi/full/10.1111/j.1600-6143.2010.03115

Thanks to Jane, whom Michael still keeps in touch with, he beat leukemia. I'd be remiss to not mention that some years later, my sister Kirsten donated one of her own kidneys to someone suffering from kidney failure. I'm not big on needles, so let's consider this book my altruistic act.

So, what's the big idea in all of this? In order to find things you deeply care about—and help your people to find what they care deeply about—look *outward*.

How can you use your talents and your career to contribute to others around you?

Whom can you serve? And what impact can you uniquely have on them?

Think about the times in your own life when you felt the greatest sense of purpose. In those moments, were you focused on yourself, or on others?

Yale professor Amy Wrzesniewski studied hospital custodial staff to understand what made the best custodians excel. It is an interesting test group given that the usual daily grind of hospital janitorial staff consists of plenty of less glamorous responsibilities such as replacing bedpans and cleaning up vomit. But Wrzesniewski found something distinctly different about those who most excelled in this line of work:

> "These custodial workers *focused intensely on serving patients*. They would '[create] the work they wanted to do out of the work they'd been assigned—work they found meaningful and worthwhile.' One would rearrange artwork in rooms to stimulate comatose patients' brains; others devoted time to learning about the chemicals they used for cleaning rooms and figuring out which were least likely to irritate patients' conditions. They were pursuing excellence in service to others and would adapt their jobs to suit that purpose. They enhanced their assigned work to be meaningful to themselves and to those they serve."[34]

These janitors took the idea of "job crafting" that we discussed earlier—in the context of doing more of what invigorates you—a step further. In addition to

---

[34] John Coleman, "To Find Meaning in Your Work, Change How You Think About It," *Harvard Business Review*, December 29, 2017, https://hbr.org/2017/12/to-find-meaning-in-your-work-change-how-you-think-about-it.

reenvisioning and expanding the responsibilities that they took on as part of the scope of their role—rearranging artwork and the like—they found ways to imbue the activities they were doing in their work with deep personal meaning by "focusing intensely on [serving others]."

This is a living, breathing example of the truism that I shared earlier: *at the most elemental level, businesses are nothing more than people working with other people to do stuff for more people.* Whether directly or indirectly, there is a person at the other end of each job that we do, and therefore, an opportunity to serve within every job. The work we do can be so much more gratifying, not to mention effective, when we focus ourselves outward on how we can maximally contribute to the betterment of that person's life.

It is no surprise that work by Wharton professor and researcher Adam Grant found that among a survey of two million workers across countless jobs and industries, those who rate their jobs as "meaningful" tend to see their jobs as a way to help others.

The whole idea of a business is predicated on helping someone—a customer—in some way that is valuable to them. And when we help them in a way that is valuable, they are willing to pay us their hard-earned money. At its most rudimentary, this is how virtually any business functions.

So, whom does your company help? What if you purposely redirect your focus from your bottom line to the ways in which you, your team, and your company serves those people? When we do this, the research—and my firsthand experience—shows that there's a good chance you'll not only find greater fulfillment and meaning in the work that you do, but you will also have a greater chance of succeeding as a business. In this way, *purpose pays*—on more than one level.

DISCOVER WHAT BRINGS YOU MEANING

Viktor Frankl pioneered a new method of therapy called logotherapy, which uses a technique he called "dereflection," a process of redirecting our attention away from excessive self-concern, and toward something outside of ourselves. He observed that we tend to get so preoccupied with ourselves—how we look, what other people think of us, whether we are good enough—that we lose sight of what really brings us fulfillment. And we sabotage our own happiness and success in the process.

Some of us have probably experienced this in the context of public speaking. When our attention stays on ourselves—"Am I making sense?" "Is the audience still with me?" "Do I have something stuck in my teeth?"—we weaken the connection with our audience because we have taken our attention away from serving them and put the attention back on ourselves. But, as a communication coach of mine once emphatically reminded me: "This isn't about you!" It is a perfectly human tendency to keep our center of focus on ourselves and our performance, but it can be the difference between totally nailing the speech and utterly face-planting.

I sure can speak to this from personal experience. You try keeping your attention focused on serving an audience of eighty MBA students while sporting a massive coffee stain down the front of your freshly pressed white shirt.

The point of dereflection is this: *in order to discover what brings us meaning, we should search outside of ourselves.*

Any discussion of "meaning" can start to seem ethereal or even intimidating—the sort of "fluffy people stuff" many leaders shy away from. It can feel lofty, which compels some to take a pilgrimage to a monastery in Nepal in search of a magical lightning strike of enlightenment. You don't need to travel that far though.

You simply need to *pause* and trace back your life and your decisions a bit, and help your people do the same as a means of finding the purpose that fuels their Blue Flame. Borrowing from the wisdom of researcher Laura King, "People don't need to know how to make their lives meaningful. They need to know *that they already are.*"[35]

In Chapter 11, I will provide an example of how to have a conversation with your people that can help them to get in closer touch with what they care most deeply about. But here are the door-opening questions that you can start with:

Whom do you feel most connected to? What is meaningful about them?
And what do you feel most connected to? What is meaningful about it?
What suffering do you care most deeply about alleviating in the world?

---

[35] Kira M. Newman, "Three Surprising Insights about Success and Happiness," *Greater Good Magazine*, July 27, 2017, https://greatergood.berkeley.edu/article/item/three_surprising_insights_about_success_and_happiness.

CONNECT YOUR WORK TO SOMETHING MUCH BIGGER

In May 1961, President John F. Kennedy stood before Congress and convinced the American people that, in order to win a cutthroat space race with the Soviet Union, the country "should commit itself to achieving the goal, before this decade is out, of landing a man on the moon and returning him safely to the Earth."

He explained months later that the goal serves "to organize and measure the best of our energies and skills, because that challenge is one that we are willing to accept, one we are unwilling to postpone, and one we intend to win."

To President Kennedy, this was about more than the importance of advancing space science. It was about uniting and rallying a nation, and unleashing the greatest talents of his fellow Americans in pursuit of a mission that was far more challenging and important than many had taken part in before. Although spaceflight doesn't seem as outlandish today, in 1961, the idea of landing a man on the moon and returning him safely seemed pretty nuts by many accounts.

Kennedy's vision gave rise to the Apollo space program, which he made a habit of visiting frequently in Houston. As legend has it, on one such trip, he took a wrong turn as he was walking to his next stop at the facility. He ended up in a service corridor where he noticed a janitor who was cleaning his mop.

Kennedy said, "Hi, I'm Jack Kennedy," as if the guy wouldn't have known without his clarification. "What do you do here?"

The janitor replied, "Well, Mr. President, *I'm helping put a man on the moon.*"

In order to discover what brings us meaning, we should search outside of ourselves.

In order to achieve their fantastical goal, each person at NASA needed to understand how their role connected to the effort of putting a man on the moon. To the custodian, he looked past the immediate tasks he was performing to the larger effort that he was contributing to. His job was about something much bigger than keeping things spick-and-span.

There is "something bigger" at play for all of us—in a similar way to how the hospital custodians from earlier recognized that their job wasn't just about ensuring the rooms stayed well kept, but about compassionately serving others who really depended on it. Oftentimes, in the heat of day-to-day battle in our jobs, we lose sight of what the work we are doing is actually all about. Sometimes, like the PIPOs at Initech, we haven't drawn the faintest connection to it in the first place.

As leaders, it is our responsibility to help draw a vivid, straight-line connection between the work that our teammates are doing and the greater good it serves. When we help them to understand this connection, the impact on their happiness and ultimately the company's results can be huge.

In the way that the moon mission of the 1960s rallied an entire nation, this "something bigger" can be a daunting but inspiring challenge. But it doesn't have to be grandiose to be meaningful.

I recall meeting Jennifer, an admissions counselor at an education company that our firm was considering investing in. We were going around the conference room table making the obligatory introductions to kick off a due diligence meeting. "Jerry, director of operations. Pleased to meet you." "Robin, vice president of marketing. Happy to be here." And around it went.

As it swung around to Jennifer, she caught us by surprise. "Hello! I'm Jennifer. I help our students to find the career of their dreams!" Jennifer's CEO quickly piped in to redirect his colleague, who had clearly broken the name and title protocol. "And your title?" he said. Jennifer retorted, a bit befuddled, "Uhhh … vice president of … dreams?"

Naturally, I was plenty intrigued by Jennifer, who, even in a brief introduction, seemed to ooze purpose. Over lunch later, I asked her to tell me more about what she did. I was conditioned to expect a rundown of her responsibilities in the way that most people customarily describe the job they do, but Jennifer was clearly different.

"What I do is pretty straightforward, Dan. I get up in the morning to help students—who have all of the potential in the world but often just need some steering—to find the career of their dreams. And when I have done that, I help them to find the right springboard—usually a school—to help launch them into that career. I don't mean to boast, but my work can create the difference between an enriching career and a humdrum one."

I purposely asked a clichéd executive question, just to see what she would say. "That's all great and really inspiring, but how does this turn into profit for the company?"

"Listen, some of them end up enrolling at our school, many do not. But I figure that if I continue to focus on understanding their hopes and dreams, and helping to guide them down the right career path for them, the ones who were meant to come to our school will end up here, and in the end, the revenue will take care of itself." And it did. Remember the idea that people perform better when they can draw the connection between what they do and how it impacts others? Jennifer, it turned out, was the biggest producer for the company.

Jennifer saw so vividly how her work connected to the bigger picture that her job was no longer just about executing the activities associated with "admissions counseling." Her real job was helping students to fundamentally create a better life. And furthermore, she understood that her job wasn't only about producing revenue for her company. It was about helping young people to discover their dream, and equipping them with the guidance to make a well-reasoned decision on how to get there, one that could have a big downstream impact on their lives—and by extension, our world.

This was powerful stuff.

> **ACTIONABLE: GET PERSPECTIVE**
>
> A simple way to help your team to discover deeper meaning in their work—like Jennifer had—is to guide them through a review of the tasks that they do each day. Use the elevating questions below to help them discover how their role is affecting "something bigger." Help them to make this connection vivid so every task is imbued with a larger meaning.
>
> • Who in the world is benefiting from what you do each day? How?
> • What impact does it have on them when you're bringing your best stuff?
> • What does it feel like to them?

We have covered a lot of ground when it comes to the three forces that comprise the Blue Flame: *what you can do best, what most invigorates you,* and *what you care deeply about*. Your talents, your passions, and your purpose, respectively. We have looked at each in isolation. But as I sense you are beginning to realize, in reality, these three forces don't exist in isolation. They are highly interrelated, and mutually reinforcing.

Let me illustrate.

As you know by now, I love playing guitar—it is creative, challenging, and collaborative. It is an activity that I find to be highly invigorating. As a result, whenever I have a spare twenty minutes, I grab my ax and riff for a bit. As you might expect, the more time I spend tightening up my scales, learning new chord progressions, and fiddling around with new solo techniques, the better I get. And the better I get, the more fun it seems to become!

We talked about the virtuous cycle that can form between talents and passions earlier. A thing called self-determination theory helps to explain why our passion seems to increase alongside our mastery. Businessman and reputed *Shark Tank* shark Mark Cuban offers a great layperson's perspective on this interplay between our talents and our passion:

> "The things I ended up being really good at were the things I found myself putting effort into. A lot of people talk about passion, but that's really not what you need to focus on. You really need to evaluate and say, 'Okay, where am I putting in my time? Because when you look at where you put in your time, where you put in your effort, that tends to be the things that you are good at. And if you put in enough time, you tend to get really good at it. If you put in enough time, and you get really good, I will give you a little secret: Nobody quits anything they are good at because it is fun to be good. It is fun to be one of the best."[36]

Use these mutually reinforcing talents and passions in a way that brings you a real sense of purpose, and voila, you have found your Blue Flame.

I will help you tie it all up with a bow at the end of the next chapter, but my sincere hope is that at this point, you have not only come much closer to understanding your own Blue Flame, but are starting to feel armed with the background, the tools, and the powerful questions to help your people find theirs. As you know by now, when you are able to do this, it can ignite a world of possibility for your people, your team, and your company.

But as you start to find your Blue Flame—and help your people discover theirs—you are faced with an important question: *how can you use your Blue Flame in a way that can have the greatest impact on your company, your community, and the world?*

---

[36] Mark Cuban, "Core Truths for Entrepreneurship," Amazon.com, https://www.amazon.com/Mark-Cuban-Insights-for-Entrepreneurs/b?ie=UTF8&node=17395090011.

IN CASE YOU MISSED IT: THE KEY IDEAS

Give the People What They Want: The research on purpose in the workplace is astounding. In a nutshell, our people are yearning for purpose—to do work that is meaningful—but few are finding it. And they want a sense of purpose so badly that they are willing to trade part of their income for it, and give up to 40 percent more discretionary effort when they find it.

Business Is Personal: At the most elemental level, businesses exist to serve other people. And human biology and psychology teach us that humans derive great pleasure and fulfillment from helping others. By creating the connection between the work that people do and the people it serves, we can imbue work with meaning.

Purpose Pays: When we make work meaningful in this way, the research teaches us that employees are more committed to their job, have higher job satisfaction, and perform better than other employees. The business benefits in helping employees find purpose in their work—not to mention the emotional and social benefits—are significant.

Leaders Lead: As leaders, we have an important responsibility to help draw a vivid, straight-line connection between the work that our teammates are doing and the greater good that it serves. When we help them to see this connection, the impact on their happiness and ultimately the company's results can be huge.

Look Outward: In order to help our employees to discover what they deeply care about—things they find deeply meaningful and gratifying—invite them to look outward. Ask, "How can you use your talents and your career to contribute to others around you? Whom do you care most deeply about, and how can you serve them? What impact can you uniquely have on them?"

Homing In: Once you have discovered what brings you a sense of purpose—and brought your talents and passions back into the picture—you will start to better understand your Blue Flame. But merely discovering your Blue Flame isn't what this is all about. At this juncture, you are faced with an important question: *How can you use your Blue Flame in a way that will have the greatest impact on your company, your community, and the world?*

Into Action

CHAPTER 10

Put a Ding in the Universe

"Many people die with their music still in them. Why is this so? Too often it is because they are always getting ready to live. Before they know it, time runs out."

— **Oliver Wendell Holmes**

My wife, who is a practicing radiation oncologist, deals each day with people who face a very uncertain—and, in many cases, bleak—outlook. Everyday reminders of human mortality are part of the gig in her line of work. After long weekdays at work, our dinner table conversations often go something like this:

Me: "How was your day?"

Her: "Umm. It was tough, but okay. Let's see ... this morning, I had to tell an otherwise normal and healthy thirty-two-year-old mother of three that she has stage four ovarian cancer. That wasn't great. Oh, but then I saw one of my favorite patients who is on the upswing from what was initially a really grim diagnosis. Later on, I held the hand of one of my terminal patients—who we worry we'll lose in a matter of days—as he cried about wishing he had been a better father to his daughter. Hmm, and come to think of it, I guess it was such a busy and consuming day that I forgot to eat lunch!"

She ravenously shovels dinner into her mouth while I sit speechless, mouth agape.

These conversations are sobering and saddening, but important reminders that life is precious and impermanent.

I hate to be the bearer of such morose news—especially now as we have made it so far through the uplifting land of talents, passions, and purpose together—but you, too, will die.

Yes ... you.

It could be at any time, really. In twenty years, in twenty months, or in twenty minutes.

And despite your wishful thinking, tomorrow is far from a given. In fact, there are roughly 2,700 people in the US alone—ordinary people like you and me—who went to bed last night thinking that tomorrow was guaranteed ... and who didn't live to see the end of today.[37]

Pope Paul VI reminded us that, in a way, we are already dying. "Somebody should tell us, right at the start of our lives, that we are dying," he said. "Then we might live life to the limit, every minute of every day. Do it! I say. Whatever you want to do, do it now! There are only so many tomorrows."

And while it's certain we will die, it's entirely unlikely that we should exist in the first place! The fact that we each were born is astonishing in itself. In fact, it is damn close to being a total statistical impossibility.

Life is precious and impermanent. Researcher and author Dr. Ali Binazir did the math—factoring together the probability of your mother meeting your father, and the probability of that single "you" sperm among its millions of buddies finding and winning the heart of the one magical egg. When you run it through the magic number machine, the actual probability of you existing at all comes out to 1 in $10^{2,685,000}$—that's a 10 followed by 2,685,000 zeroes.[38]

It looks like this:

1,000,000,000,000,000,000,000,000,000,000,000,000,000,000,000,000,
000,000,000,000,000,000,000,000,000,000,000,000,000,000,000,000,
000,000,000,000,000,000,000,000,000,000,000,000,000,000,000,000,
000,000,000,000,000,000,000,000,000,000,000,000,000,000,000,000,
000,000,000,000,000,000,000000,000,000,000,000,000,000,000,000,
000,000,000,000,000,000,000,000,000,000,000,000,000,000,000,000,
000,000,000,000,000,000,000,000,000,000,000,000,000,000,000,000,
000,000,000,000,000,000,000,000,000,000,000,000,000,000,000,000,
000,000,000,000,000,000,000,000,000,000,000,000,000,000,000,000,
000,000,000,000,000,000,000,000,000,000,000,000,000,000,000,000,
000,000,000,000,000,000,000,000,000,000,000,000,000,000,000,000,
000,000,000,000,000,000,000,000,000,000,000,000,000,000,000,000,

---

[37] "How Many People Die in the USA Every Day?" Quora.com, April 30, 2020, https://www.quora.com/How-many-people-die-in-the-USA-every-day.
[38] Dina Spector, "The Odds of You Being Alive Are Incredibly Small," *Business Insider*, June 11, 2012, https://www.businessinsider.com/infographic-the-odds-of-being-alive-2012-6.

000,000,000,000,000,000,000,000,000,000,000,000,000,000,000,000,000,000,
000,000,000,000,000,000,000,000000,000,000,000,000,000,000,000,000,000,
000,000,000,000,000,000,000,000,000,000,000,000,000,000,000,000,000,000,
000,000,000,000,000,000,000,000,000,000,000,000,000,000,000,000,000,000,
000,000,000,000,000,000,000,000,000,000,000,000,000,000,000,000,000,000,
000,000,000,000,000,000,000,000,000,000,000,000,000,000,000,000,000,000,
000,000,000,000,000,000,000,000,000,000,000,000,000,000,000,000,000,000,
000,000,000,000,000,000,000,000,000,000,000,000,000,000,000,000,000,000,
000,000,000,000,000,000,000,000,000,000,000,000,000,000,000,000,000,000,
000,000,000,000,000,000,000,000,000,000,000,000,000,000,000,000,000,000,
000,000,000,000,000,000,000,000,000,000,000,000,000,000,000,000,000,000,
000,000,000,000,000,000,000,000,000,000,000,000,000,000,000,000,000,000,
000,000,000,000,000,000,000,000,000,000,000,000,000,000,000,000,000,000,
000,000,000,000,000,000,000,000,000,000,000,000,000,000,000,000,000,000,
000,000,000,000,000,000,000,000,000,000,000,000,000,000,000000,000,
000,000,000,000,000,000,000,000,000,000,000,000,000,000,000,000,000,000,
000,000,000,000,000,000,000,000,000,000,000,000,000,000,000,000,000,000,
000,000,000,000,000,000,000,000,000,000,000,000,000,000,000,000,000,000,
000,000,000,000,000,000,000,000,000,000,000,000,000,000,000,000,000,000,
000,000,000,000,000,000,000,000000,000,000,000,000,000,000,000,000,000,
000,000,000,000,000,000,000,000,000,000,000,000,000,000,000,000,000,000,
000,000,000,000,000,000,000,000,000,000,000,000,000,000,000,000,000,000,
000,000,000,000,000,000,000,000,000,000,000,000,000,000,000,000,000,000,
000,000,000,000,000,000,000,000,000,000,000,000,000,000,000,000,000,000,
000,000,000,000,000,000,000,000,000,000,000,000,000,000,000,000,000,000,
000,000,000,000,000,000,000,000,000,000,000,000,000,000,000,000,000,000,
000,000,000,000,000,000,000,000,000,000,000,000,000,000,000,000,000,000,
000,000,000,000,000,000,000,000,000,000,000,000,000,000,000,000,000,000,
000,000,000,000,000,000,000,000,000000,000,000,000,000,000,000,000,000,
000,000,000,000,000,000,000,000,000,000,000,000,000,000,000,000,000,000,
000,000,000,000,000,000,000,000,000,000,000,000,000,000,000,000,000,000,
000,000,000,000,000,000,000,000,000,000,000,000,000,000,000,000,000,000,
000,000,000,000,000,000,000,000,000,000,000,000,000,000,000,000,000,000,
000,000,000,000,000,000,000,000,000,000,000,000,000,000,000,000,000,000,
000,000,000,000,000,000,000,000,000,000,000,000,000,000,000,000,000,000,
000,000,000,000,000,000,000,000,000,000,000,000,000,000,000,000,000...
(and a bunch more zeroes after that).

The translation? Statistically speaking, the odds of you existing are basically ... zero. Zilch.

Next time your mom gloats that you are "one in a million," you can thank her for the well-intentioned compliment, but correct her mathematical inaccuracy. She's way off.

To put this massive improbability into context, if you were flying over the US and threw a Ping-Pong ball out the window, there is a higher chance it would land in a bucket that was randomly placed somewhere in the US.

From another angle, the probability of you having been born is lower than blindly guessing the exact order of a deck of playing cards—five times in a row.

But however improbable it is that we exist in the first place, the probability that we will die is 100 percent.

When we understand this—when we truly internalize how finite life is, and how fortunate we are to have a shot at it in the first place—it raises a very important, existential question, the one elegantly posed by poet Mary Oliver: "*What is it you plan to do with your one wild and precious life?*"

(I know: I just fed you a lot of heavy, existential stuff. So take a minute to chew before you swallow and proceed to the next bite.)

In this same vein, in his 2005 commencement speech at Stanford University—a few years before he died of cancer—Steve Jobs drew on the perspective that his own dance with death gave him to help graduates understand a fundamental truth:

> "Remembering that I'll be dead soon is the most important tool I've ever encountered to help me make the big choices in life. Because almost everything—all external expectations, all pride, all fear of embarrassment or failure—these things just fall away in the face of death, leaving only what is truly important."

Normally, commencement speeches center around an uplifting, feel-good topic like "You have the power to change the world." But heck, this was Steve Jobs, he could talk about what he had for breakfast and everyone would still be impressed. He continued:

"For the past thirty-three years, I have looked in the mirror every morning and asked myself: 'If today were the last day of my life, would I want to do what I am about to do today?' And whenever the answer has been 'no' for too many days in a row, I know I need to change something."[39]

Many of us don't think about death much, or at all. And even fewer of us use it as a motivating force, as Mary Oliver's quote encourages us to. It often gets lost on us that being alive today—reading this book in this moment—is a nearly impossible coincidence. Some might even call it a miracle.

But in the same way that Jobs does in his modern-day commencement speech, the Stoics have been imploring us to keep death front-of-mind for ages now.

What is it you plan to do with your one wild and precious life?

Stoicism—an ancient Greek school of philosophy founded by Zeno of Citium—is centered around the development of self-control, acceptance, and emotional resilience as a means of overcoming destructive emotions. The philosophy asserts that contentment in life comes by way of learning to make the best of our situation, no matter the circumstances.

Stoicism has stood the test of time, its devotees including: George Washington, Theodore Roosevelt, Abraham Lincoln, Seattle Seahawks coach Pete Carroll, and rapper T-Pain.

T-Pain even raps about it: "Asphyxiation got me losin' my brain. She's my grim reaper. I'm in love with death."

A central tenet of the Stoic philosophy is "memento mori," which translates roughly into "remember that you must die."

Remember death? Embrace death? Or even "love" death, like T-Pain claims to? "Who would want to do that?" you might be asking. And I get it. We often consider contemplating death to be morbid or depressing. But it doesn't have to be. As the Stoics taught, remembering our mortality is the key that unlocks greater meaning in life, and a greater zest for living. As Stoic Marcus Aurelius

---

[39] Steve Jobs, "Text of Steve Jobs' Commencement Address," *Stanford News*, June 12, 2005, https://news.stanford.edu/2005/06/14/jobs-061505/.

said, "You could leave life right now. Let that determine what you do and say and think."

Being able to see life in relation to our own mortality—the reality that life will inevitably end—puts a lot into perspective. It makes you realize how inconsequential the passive-aggressive glare from that knucklehead who honked at you on the highway was. It makes it seem silly to lose sleep over the ego-crushing constructive critique your boss had for you after this afternoon's presentation. It makes it seem insignificant that the dog chose to relieve himself on the living room carpet, even though it's easy to get ticked off in the moment. When we fail to see the bigger picture, choosing instead to let ourselves be consumed by minutiae like these, we start to miss the point.

The truth is, as you surely know when you stop to think about it, life isn't about answering emails and hitting productivity goals either. It isn't even about delivering on financial results. Sure, I have emphasized the value that the Blue Flame can deliver to your business—the real dollar-and-cent value. And I have gone to great lengths to offer a well-reasoned argument that this Blue Flame thing is exactly what you need to take your leadership, and your company, to the next level. But it is time we look at all of this from a much higher altitude. From that level, we can see that using the Blue Flame strictly as a means of getting more performance out of our people also misses kind of the point.

At the deepest level, the Blue Flame is about living richer, more impactful lives by leaning into our talents, our passions, and our purpose. In the words of the Ikigai tradition, the Blue Flame—in its most essential form—is about creating *a life worth living.* And *work that is worth spending our life doing.*

And it just so happens that when we do this, all sorts of other amazing things tend to happen—including, but certainly not limited to, enhanced business results.

There's lots to chew on here. Personally, when I sit with all of this, I find myself having three feelings:

First, *holy smokes.* If my mom and my dad hadn't happened to have been playing darts next to each other in that musty college bar in the early '70s, I wouldn't be here. And if Dad's parents hadn't met on that cold night in 1944 in Chicago and happened to strike up a conversation, he wouldn't be here, and so on, and so on. *#MindBlown* 🤯

Second, I am struck with a profound sense of appreciation that through whatever combination of biology, coincidence, and divine intervention, I was born in this era to these parents, and with the opportunity and good fortune that I've had. *#Gratitude* 🙏

And third, I'm struck with a strong sense of responsibility to *make my life count*. To make it stand for something. To invest myself in things that are important. To make an imprint—however big or small—on the world that I'll one day leave behind. As Steve Jobs said, to "put a ding in the universe." *#UniverseDing* 🔔🌎

BACK TO THE FUTURE

Imagine for a moment that you manage to borrow the keys to Doc Brown and Marty McFly's DeLorean. You fire that puppy up for your long-awaited chance to experience time travel, and the flux capacitor is set to the future date of your retirement—whenever that might be for you.

Be sure to pack some antidepressants, as seeing your aged self could be jarring. I can only assume that what little bit is left of my hairline will have been totally decimated by then.

On that long-anticipated retirement date, imagine that you step out of the DeLorean and arrive at your retirement party. Take a moment and really start to envision it.

Where is your retirement party? Mine is at a casual pizza place that serves cold beer.

Who is gathered there to celebrate? Whom do you hope to see there? When I envision mine, it is chock-full of colleagues, customers, family, teachers, and students. Standing room only, I hope.

You settle into the soiree, feeling grateful and honored, but a bit overwhelmed by the turnout. You feel that awkward mix of deep pride and bashful undeservedness.

Amid the casual mixing and mingling, you are the subject of countless stories that are shared. Some funny ones. Some heavier ones. Some embarrassing ones. Each adds its own texture to what was, as you are reminded, an incredibly rich career—one full of ups and downs, obstacles and triumphs, laughter and tears.

And as the night wears on, you are able to start to see the meta-view of your career a bit more clearly. You are able to see what it was all about in a higher-fidelity way than ever before. It wasn't about maintaining a perfect batting average on key decisions. You nailed some, and you whiffed mightily on others. It wasn't about being the smartest. There were surely smarter people you encountered along the way. It wasn't about everyone liking you, as you recognize that making tough decisions didn't always make you popular.

But ultimately, you conclude, the measure of a career is determined by a simple but essential question: Did I use my gifts and talents in a way that was both deeply personally fulfilling and maximized my impact on those who I served? On my teammates ... my company(s) ... my customers ... my community ... our world?

The Blue Flame—in its most essential form—is about creating a life worth living.

As you're reflecting on this, from within the cacophony of casual conversation, you hear that unmistakable sound of a butter knife faintly tapping on a wine glass. You see others reaching for their glassware, gearing up for the open toast segment of the evening's celebration.

Recognizing the gravity of the moment—the chance to understand the true impact you have had on those in your orbit during your career—you tune in.

Just imagine for a moment: *What will others say about you at your retirement party?*

About what you did? Who you were?

What will they say about the ways in which you led?

What will they say about what they learned from you?

What will they share about the achievements you've enjoyed?

About how you showed up during the tough times?

What will they say about the impact you had? On them personally ... on the companies you served ... on the world?

Fundamentally, as you ride off into the sunset, how do you want those who mattered most to you to remember the mark you made?

When all is said and done, how have you applied your Blue Flame—your talents, your passions, and your purpose—in a way that "put a ding in the universe"?

YOUR AREA OF GREATEST IMPACT

This exercise, a powerful retrospective, encourages us to wrestle with a question whose importance is paramount to a life well lived and a career well served: *Where can I apply my talents, passions, and purpose to have the greatest impact while I'm here?*

I call this your *area of greatest impact*. And it doesn't have to be singular. Think about how you can use your Blue Flame to have a big, universe-dinging impact on your career. On your family. On your community. On the world.

Getting clear on my own Blue Flame led me to identify one of the areas where I could have the greatest impact: American workplaces. This is an area where my Blue Flame—my talents, my passions, and my purpose—can be applied to have what I hope will be a big impact. You'll start to understand, then, why I wrote this book.

As you are reflecting on your own area of greatest impact—and as a leader, guiding your teammates through the same—here are a few important ideas I want to encourage you to consider:

Play big: As architect Daniel H. Burnham said, "Make no little plans; they have no magic to stir men's blood. ... Make big plans, aim high in hope and work." Life is precious, short, and uncertain. And we only get one shot at it. The world needs us to "make big plans."

Borrowing from the wisdom of technologist Tim O'Reilly, "What is something that is so important that even if you fail, the world is better off with you having tried?"

Breaking the color barrier in American professional sports was so important to Jackie Robinson, he was willing to risk everything and endure relentless racial attacks. The world is way better off with him having tried.

More recently, Malala Yousafzai called on her talent and passion for writing and expression to pen a then-anonymous diary about what life was like under Taliban rule. Giving oppressed women a voice and fighting on their behalf for the right to an education were supremely important to her. The world is way better off with her having tried.

Committing ourselves to something big, something this important, calls forth our best stuff.

Think expansively: In most cases, our current company (let alone our current role) is such a tiny sliver of the larger canvas on which we have the chance to paint our Blue Flame. Exploring your area of greatest impact only at your current company is like looking at the vast and boundless night sky through a pinhole. The world is a big place, its needs are diverse and broad, and the opportunities to have an impact are endless. When thinking about your area of greatest impact, think expansively, not narrowly. Think globally, not locally.

For leaders like you who are guiding these conversations, this can seem daunting, as it isn't often that conversations of this magnitude happen in the workplace. It can also feel like a risky proposition. "Why would I want to lead someone away from staying with our company? Finding great people is tough!" you're wondering. It's true: good talent is tough to come by, and expensive to retain.

> **How do you want those who mattered most to you to remember the mark you made?**

But what if it turns out someone's unique combination of talents, passions, and purpose aren't actually needed by your organization? Or what if your organization doesn't present the greatest opportunity for them to maximize their impact—to put their ding in the universe? Does it really make sense to keep them around if it means suppressing their Blue Flame? Are you taking a stand strictly for business results, or are you willing to take a stand to help the people whom you have been charged to lead to live their most impactful life and burn brightly in the world—even if it means going in a new direction?

Stay fluid: Our Blue Flames, and where we can apply them to have the greatest impact, will evolve over time as we learn, grow, and gain wisdom. Stay open to learning new things about yourself, and how you can use those new insights to navigate toward your areas of greatest impact.

TYING IT ALL TOGETHER

We have covered lots of ground. You'll recall early on, we discussed that although this Blue Flame concept is simple on its surface—do what you're good at, what brings you passion, and what gives you a sense of meaning—as you have come to appreciate, there's a bit more than meets the eye. You now understand how vague advice like "follow your passion" or "lean into your strengths" needs to be explored at a deeper level, rather than taken at face value and followed strictly and literally.

But for all of the complexity that sits beneath the surface of these seemingly simple ideas, we return right back to where we started.

Committing ourselves to something big, something this important, calls forth our best stuff.

Amazing things can indeed happen when people play at the intersection point of three powerful forces: *what they can do best, the activities that invigorate them, and what they care deeply about.* I'm convinced, and I hope you are too, that lives can be profoundly richer, teams and companies can be demonstrably more successful, and the world can be a markedly better place if we leaders lean into our own Blue Flames, and accept the calling to help those whom we lead to find theirs.

With all of the exploration, soul-searching, and self-inquiry that this book is intended to spark around the idea of the Blue Flame, it's time for a return to "simplicity on the other side of complexity."

In 1962, President Kennedy was joined at the White House for dinner by Congresswoman Clare Boothe Luce. When he asked her what was on her mind, she hesitantly but courageously told him that her fear for him was that there were too many priorities competing for his attention. She reminded him that successful presidents often had a clear and specific focus.

"Mr. President, *a great person is one sentence.* Abraham Lincoln's sentence was: 'He preserved the union and freed the slaves.' Franklin Roosevelt's was: 'He lifted us out of a great depression and helped us win a world war.' What is on my mind, Mr. President, is: what sentence will describe you when you leave here?"

There's great power and clarity in brevity. By trying to be too much, or be too many things, we risk not doing enough.

ACTIONABLE: THE BLUE FLAME STATEMENT

Armed with what is hopefully a greater personal clarity as regards your talents, your passions, and your purpose, ask yourself: *What is my sentence?*

I call this the Blue Flame Statement. I have one, and you now should too.

Create it. Know it. Own it. Tell people about it. Put it on your wall. Print it out and carry it around in your pocket as your *real* ID card.

You can visit MyBlueFlame.com to download a free worksheet to help you bring this all together, or you can scribble it in the margins of this book.

Here are the raw materials you will need:

1. *What can you do best?* Boil your most potent talents down to three or four key words or phrases.
2. *What most invigorates you?* Note three or four things that you find most energizing.
3. *What do you care deeply about?* Summarize what brings you the greatest sense of purpose or meaning.
4. Finally, *where can these things—your talents, passions, and purpose—be best applied?* What will be your ding in the universe?

A great person is one sentence.

I'll offer a simple Blue Flame formula. Don't feel like you need to follow this exactly, but it should give you a good starting point for how you can meld your talents, passions, purpose, and area of greatest impact into a pithy, authentic statement that helps remind you how to lean into your Blue Flame.

With....[My Talents]...., I.... [My Passions & Purpose].... , so that....[Impact]....

Here is mine:

With creativity, persistence, and a steadfast belief in others, Dan helps to teach, equip and inspire a new generation of conscious leaders, so that families can be stronger, communities can be more vibrant, and workplaces can become a source of deep fulfillment for people everywhere.

IN CASE YOU MISSED IT: THE KEY IDEAS

It's a Miracle: The fact that each of us was born in the first place is astonishing. Statistically speaking, it's a near impossibility. Mathematically, the probability of you having been born is lower than blindly guessing the exact order of an entire deck of fifty-two playing cards … five times in a row.

Remember Death: Given that each of us was given a shot at life, we have to remember that our life is precious and impermanent. This is a central tenet of the Stoic philosophy, *memento mori,* which translates roughly into "remember that you must die." The Stoics reminded us, "You could leave life right now. Let that determine what you do and say and think."

Live Before You Die: Remembering death can create energy, vibrancy, and a motivation to *live*. As Pope Paul VI told us, "Somebody should tell us, right at the start of our lives, that we are dying. Then we might live life to the limit, every minute of every day. Do it! I say. Whatever you want to do, do it now! There are only so many tomorrows." So, ask yourself, *What is it you plan to do with your one wild and precious life?*

Make it Count: It's up to us to make life stand for something. To invest ourselves in things that are important. To make an imprint—however big or small—on the world that we'll one day leave behind. As Steve Jobs said, to "put a ding in the universe."

Not Just a Leadership Technique: When we look at the Blue Flame through this lens, it extends well beyond driving greater performance in our business. It is about seizing the opportunity to create richer lives and more rewarding and impactful workplaces. It is about the opportunity to positively impact families and communities for whatever time we do have here.

Your Turn: *What do you want others to say about you at your retirement party? About what you did? Who you were? What will they say about the ways in which you led? What will they say about what they learned from you? When all is said and done, what ding will you have made in the universe?*

CHAPTER 11

Blue Flame Conversations

My hope is that, by now, you're all-in on the performance-enhancing, life-altering, company-accelerating, world-changing potential of the Blue Flame.

At the end of the day, I believe being a great leader—the kind that gets the best out of their people—requires having clarifying, empowering, and actionable Blue Flame conversations. This chapter is meant to provide a road map for how to have these conversations. We'll use the fictional example of Alicia and her marketing manager, Joshua. I expect that parts of their story will sound familiar to you.

★ ★ ★

It was a brilliant spring day in Denver and Alicia was lucky enough to have a view of the snow-capped Rocky Mountains outside her office window. She's the head of sales and marketing for a bioinformatics company. Bioinformatics applies computer science and information engineering to data about biological processes. Her company specializes in working with pharmaceutical companies on drug design and discovery; with the energy industry on the development of clean biomass energy; and with agribusinesses to improve crop yields and disease resistance.

The company was very much in growth mode and Alicia had some stiff sales targets to hit. As things stood, her department was off-target for the year, and Alicia was feeling the pressure. She felt that her team wasn't really rising to the challenge. She planned a meeting with her marketing manager, and was in the process of getting herself mentally prepared. She owed it to her colleague to be focused and collected.

The sales and account management teams didn't feel they were getting enough support from marketing. Marketing seemed to feel they were doing all they could—and, to be fair, they were a pretty small team. But she had a nagging feeling that marketing wasn't really stepping up. They didn't seem especially engaged. There was no energy, no sparkle. Things felt a bit flat.

Joshua, the marketing manager, was bright and likable, and got on well with his colleagues. His team of four people had a lot on their plate—running the company's marketing and PR campaigns and keeping the sales and account management team supplied with marketing materials that reflected the company's most recent technical advances. It wasn't that Joshua was seriously face-planting in his role, but what Alicia had been hearing was that people felt Joshua and his team were reactive, not proactive. They weren't working at the velocity needed to support sales, or giving the account management team what they needed to more aggressively drive expansion business from major existing customers. Because of this, she felt marketing was really getting in the way of driving growth and hitting the number.

She seemed to find herself putting out fires for them all day, and losing sleep over whether they were going to get the job done.

Maybe it's time to let Joshua go, she found herself thinking. She imagined a future where she had replaced Joshua with a new marketing manager, a paragon of marketing awesomeness who brought nothing but success to Alicia's desk. She let herself enjoy that daydream for a few minutes.

But she remembered this book and reminded herself of a core belief that Blue Flame leaders hold true: *Everyone has talent, and my job is to help them discover it and use it at the point of highest impact.*

Joshua had been with the company for a few years now, and Alicia felt knowledgeable about his talents and blind spots. She and Joshua were overdue for a Blue Flame conversation. Alicia scolded herself for not having initiated one sooner, as she had committed to having Blue Flame conversations with all of her employees early in their time at the company.

Alicia's company was on a mission to bring innovative data solutions to the health, energy, and food production sectors. They were using cutting-edge data technologies—and supposedly cutting-edge thinking and creativity—to come up with answers that would make the world a better place and enrich people's lives. Alicia reminded herself that in order to do that, the first people whose lives they had a responsibility to enrich were their employees, by ensuring they found fulfilling, meaningful roles that sparked their Blue Flame.

Alicia's responsibility was to find out where she and the company were failing to help Joshua do what he could do best. *Do I have him in the wrong role? Is he not clear on what's expected? Am I not supporting him well enough? Have we failed to motivate him?*

This was a perfect time to take a big step back and revisit his Blue Flame—his talents, his passions, and his purpose—so she could help him apply those in a way that could have a bigger impact. This framing elevated the coming conversation to a new level. This wasn't about scolding Joshua. It was about going back to square one so she could figure out how to help him come alive again—and by extension, solve whatever was holding the marketing team back.

Joshua knocked on the doorframe and Alicia invited him in. She pulled out two chairs so that they were facing each other; she knew it was important to create an open and connective setting for the conversation they were about to have.

She sat down in the chair facing Joshua with her hands lightly clasped together and resting on her knees, a posture she hoped would signal openness and safety. They exchanged some pleasantries and Joshua prepared himself for what he thought would be a tactical discussion on the week's events. Instead, Alicia took a daring plunge into a Blue Flame Conversation.

> **Alicia:** Before we talk about the nitty-gritty of what's going on in the business right now, and how I can best support you, I have this hunch that one of the best ways I can support you is to use this time refocusing our energy on ... *you*.
>
> **Joshua:** Okay! That sounds great, though I feel kind of distracted with how much is going on. I'm not sure how present I can be right now.
>
> **Alicia:** I totally understand this may feel out of place given all that we have going on in the company. I just think one of the most fundamental things that I can do to help you crush it is to slow down and recenter on a simple but crucial question that I've been pondering lately. *How can we get the best out of you?* You want that. I want that. And, no doubt, the company wants that.

Alicia turned to a whiteboard where she had drawn the Blue Flame diagram with its three axes.

Alicia: Are you familiar with the Blue Flame concept?

Joshua: Yes, it's the intersection of your talents, your passions, and your purpose, right? I've heard it gives people clarity about where and how they can have the most impact. I've seen the Blue Flame Statements hanging on people's cubicles but haven't really done a deep dive.

If the person you're talking to doesn't know much about the Blue Flame, explain the following:

- Your Blue Flame is what sits at the intersection between your talents, your passions, and your purpose. When people discover what they do best, what invigorates them, and what brings them a sense of meaning, and do things that sit at the intersection of these forces, it can make people come alive and find much more meaning and fulfillment while they're doing it.

- Best of all, once the Blue Flame is lit, a leader and their teammate can work together to figure out where and how to apply it so it has the most impact.

- Ask the rhetorical question, "Can you imagine what our company would be like if everyone were operating in this sweet spot? Can you imagine what the whole world would look like? Let's be part of that change. Starting with you."

Alicia: That's great that you know the basics. I was hoping we could spend some time today discussing your Blue Flame. Have you ever thought about it?

Joshua: Not really, but I see why having some clarity could be really helpful for me and the team. I'd be happy to spend some time exploring with you if you think it would help.

Alicia: That's great, thanks for being open. Let me just take your temperature on where you are right now. Just off the cuff: When you walked into work this morning, how were you feeling on a scale of one to ten? Ten is totally lit up and ready to rock, and one is totally bummed out and ready to head right back out the door.

Joshua: Um, six? I'm happy to be here but a bit overwhelmed.

Alicia: And on an average day?

Joshua: Maybe seven?

It's important to ask this question because you want to create a shared understanding of where they are right now. There's no right or wrong answer here, so it is important to not cast judgment on their answer. Wherever they are is just fine.

Alicia: Great, now let's try something. Close your eyes. Now, visualize how life would be if you came into work every day feeling closer to a nine? Or even a ten? Can you imagine how that would feel?

Joshua: It would feel great. I'd feel on fire.

Alicia: Not only would you feel on fire, but you'd light up the whole company with your excitement! I can picture it now! Over the next hour, we're going to unpack what you're best at, what types of activities you find to be invigorating, and what you care most deeply about—which we will shorthand as talents, passions, and purpose. This should lead us in the direction of helping you to find your spark again.

1. FIND THEIR TALENTS

There are a lot of conflated terms when it comes to talent. We use words like skill, talent, predisposition, aptitude, expertise, flair, knack, and ability interchangeably. It's important to help the person you're guiding through this conversation to understand that talent is what underlies all of these things—it is the essence of one's abilities, recurring patterns of thought or behavior that tend to show up time and time again, in a variety of activities and situations. Everyone has talents, but many people struggle to understand them and see them clearly. So it is your job to help people find them, own them, and put them to good use.

Alicia: Let's start with your talents. First, to make this go more smoothly, I'd like to differentiate between talent, skills, and knowledge. For instance, I'm the head of marketing, but marketing isn't my talent, it's just a set of skills that I've acquired over time. And, if I'm any good at marketing, it's because of certain talents that have helped me learn these skills effectively.

Alica stood up to draw this on the board:

Alicia: Think of knowledge as *things you know*. In marketing, I know that if we run a marketing campaign through print media, we should expect a better than four times return on ad spend. This is based on my prior knowledge and some factual benchmarking. Then, you can think of skills as *competencies that can be learned*. For instance, I had to learn how to understand customer needs, how to create messaging and value positioning that speaks to those needs, how to create a brand proposition that resonates with the market. Those sorts of things.

Joshua: I get it, and so your talents are the foundation that underlie all of these? But how would you describe these talents?

Alicia: Exactly! It helps to think of talents as *repeated patterns of behavior or thought that can be made useful.* These patterns tend to show up time and time again in different contexts and situations, and have likely been wired into you for a while. We might need to learn various pieces of knowledge and skills, but our core *talents* are what underpin everything.

Joshua: That all makes sense. As head of marketing, what talents underly your marketing skills?

It's important for a leader to be open, vulnerable, and authentic in Blue Flame conversations. Doing so will ensure the person you're speaking to feels safe to open up as well. Don't make this conversation about you, but freely use yourself as an example to explain the key concepts.

Alicia: So, for me, I'm really good with numbers and analytics, my brain just understands them on a deep level and is highly *analytical*. This has come in handy for the analytical elements of what we do, like performance marketing. Also, for as long as I can remember, I've been adept at putting myself in someone else's shoes. In talent-speak, I would label this *empathy*. This has enabled me to become skillful in persuasion—another one of my signature talents—because I understand how to meet people where they are, get to the heart of their needs and desires, and figure out ways for them to address those.

Understanding my talents has unlocked great opportunities for me because I understand what I can do best, and how I can apply those things in new and bigger ways.

Joshua: That all makes sense.

Alicia: Okay, your turn! What do you think you are able to do better than most other people?

To help guide this conversation, you can pull out and refer to the Blue Flame Talent Inventory, which can be accessed at MyBlueFlame.com.

Joshua: I've always thought I was good at writing. I loved English in school, and I loved creative writing in particular. In the end, I studied communications because I thought it would be more helpful in the working world.

Alicia: Yes, you *are* good at writing—you write well. I've seen that in your work. What would you say are the core talents that underpin that skill? What would you say enables you to be good at writing?

As Alicia is doing here, it is important for the leader to help drill down to the root talent. This is key because many talents can be applied in a whole host of ways in our lives. Identifying them—as opposed to strictly focusing on skills or knowledge—allows us to think more expansively about how we can best use what our brains are built to do most successfully.

Joshua: I think I have a talent with words. Maybe a talent for language is a better way to put it. I studied French and Italian at school and found that they came quite easily to me. So, understanding how a language works and how to use a language, maybe?

Alicia: That's great. You have identified something that I think they call *linguistic intelligence*.

Joshua: I think perhaps processing information, also. Maybe that's vague. I just feel like I'm good at taking a lot of information and digesting and summarizing it succinctly. That's a big part of our job in marketing.

Alicia: Ah, now, you're getting it, and starting to drill down to the *talent*. And what goes on in your brain when you're processing information in that way?

Joshua: I think my brain just has a way of seeing themes and patterns in data, and quickly inferring what they mean. I'm guessing this is why people sometimes come to me with big spreadsheets of data to help them make sense of it all. And the same thing happens with words, you know? With a whole bunch of information from reports and journal articles and so on, I can read through those and see a pretty clear summation of what's at the heart of all that. I can turn it into a compelling and articulate story.

Alicia: Yeah, I think that you're homing in on a talent called *synthesis*.

Joshua: That sounds right. Also, I'm not sure if this counts as a talent, but I think creativity is a big one. I love to create new things—stories mainly. I've always got some creative writing project in the works—just as a hobby. I'm not hoping to write the next great American novel or anything. But I do find that when I start with the germ of an idea—it could be anything, something I've seen or read or just something that pops into my head—my mind just automatically embellishes it. I have to spin it into a story.

Alicia: Well I truly hope you *do* write the next great American novel. I want a copy. I also think the talent you're describing might be *imagination*. You seem to be a very imaginative person—producing ideas out of thin air. Does that sound right?

Joshua nodded and Alicia stood up and wrote language, synthesis, *and* imagination. *She pulled out a copy of the Talents Inventory from* The Blue Flame *book and handed it to Joshua.*

Alicia: As you scan this sheet, are there any other talents that you really identify with? Here's a question that can provide a gateway to discovering your talents: What are the things that have seemed to come very naturally or easily to you in life?

Joshua: Well, I don't know if this is relevant, but I get on easily with people. I have a big network of friends and acquaintances.

Alicia added empathy *and* connectedness *to the whiteboard.*

Joshua: I've always been good at sports. Mainly skiing but also a bit of running. I skied for the Denver University ski team—the Pioneers. They're a pretty high-level team. We won the NCAA championship.

Alicia: Wow, that's amazing. But I think skiing is actually a *skill*. So, let's look for the talents that underpin that skill. What do you think was at the foundation of your skiing skill? What talents made that possible?

Joshua: Well, I have good balance but I don't think that's a talent. Most people are physically capable of skiing. So I think I would say that the talents were what allowed me to focus on what I had to do to be a very good skier. So I think focus and discipline are probably key. I needed to have a vision of what I wanted to accomplish in skiing, and I needed the focus and discipline to keep at it each day.

Alicia: Now you're getting the hang of it. Focus and discipline are great talents that set you apart from others and probably come up again and again regardless of what you're doing. So, look at your talent axis of the Blue Flame. You have language, synthesis, imagination, empathy, connectedness, focus, and discipline. How does this all feel so far?

Joshua: It looks good, and it feels nice to identify. It feels pretty true to life. I haven't thought about them in quite that light before.

Alicia: It's counterintuitive, but, in general, humans aren't all that good at seeing our own talents. But usually it starts to become apparent if you take the time to look, and are able to drill beneath the surface to search for the underlying talents. For instance, you have probably had a bunch of performance reviews with your prior bosses, right?

Joshua: Yep.

Alicia: It is important to couple your own perspective with outside perspective. You know, from performance reviews, 360-degree reviews, and even just conversations with those who know you best. See, we humans struggle to see ourselves completely objectively. We overestimate our talent in some places, and underestimate it in others. This is just a part of being human. So if you draw on the external perspective from reviews and such, and look at your list of talents, how would you rank them by how often they come up from other people's perspective?

Joshua: *Creativity* is definitely at the top. Most people I've worked with have often talked about how I'm at my best when I am doing things that are creative—making things, building things, envisioning new things. And after that comes *empathy* and *connectedness*. My managers have tended to say that I'm good at working with people; that I quickly forge good, connective working relationships. They say that I'm a great listener and can understand other people well. I suppose people also bring up my synthesis abilities from time to time. People don't tend to mention *language* so much, because I think that's below the surface. And my skiing coach used to say I was very *focused* and *disciplined*—but my work managers not so much.

Alicia stepped away from the whiteboard and sat across from Joshua.

Alicia: Part of my role as your leader is to notice where I see you at your best, and help you to see what I see. So, do you mind if I add my own thoughts here?

Joshua: Of course not.

Alicia: I would rank creativity, empathy, and synthesis atop my list, as well. But I would add something that I think you might be overlooking because it probably seems like second nature to you. You are energetic, and when I've seen you working with your team, there are times when everyone seems to be humming—working with an intensity that I think comes from the tone you set. When you are leveraging this natural energy, you are clearly capable of giving strong direction and leadership. I sense that the team knows exactly what needs to be done, and what they have to do to achieve it ... and you're able to get the team really fired up to go get it done.

Joshua: Thank you!

Alicia: There's a bit of a caveat here, though. I don't *always* see energy in you, or your team. In the same way it's my job as a leader to help you find your Blue Flame and flourish, it's also your job as a team leader to help everyone on your team move toward their Blue Flame. It's nothing horrible, but I have heard some feedback that suggests that the marketing team could use some more energy. I hear you all are doing exactly what is being asked of you, but little more.

Joshua: Oh.

Alicia: Don't worry. That's what we're here for today. My point is that you have the capacity, the *talent*, to get your team fired up and focused—I've seen it myself. So, today we'll explore all the ways we can get you and your team fired up more consistently. As long as you feel like it fits, I'm going to add *enrolling* to your list of talents, because I think you really do have a talent for bringing people with you, getting them on board.

Now, at the end of the first chapter of their Blue Flame conversation, the whiteboard had listed:

1. *Language*
2. *Synthesis***
3. *Imagination*
4. *Empathy***
5. *Connectedness***
6. *Focus*
7. *Discipline*
8. *Creativity***
9. *Energetic***
10. *Enrolling*

Alicia: Look at this. You're a talented guy! As we discussed, some of these are more prominent and potent than others, so I'm going to star the top five things we've homed in on as your "signature talents." Don't worry—this isn't cast in stone anywhere. It will just help us to see the forest through the trees here. Remember, this discussion is not about helping you find what you can do *okay* or even *sufficiently well*. It is about helping you find what you can do *best*.

2. FIND THEIR PASSIONS

Next up, you shift your attention to discovering your teammate's passions. This can be found in the activities that they find most invigorating. Ones that give them energy, light them up, and put them "in the zone." There is a good chance they have a sense of what creates that passionate feeling—especially when they stop to think about the types of activities that have given them this feeling before—but perhaps they don't really see how it connects to their job. But other than bingeing The Office, *everyone's passions will have some applicability to the workplace.*

Alicia: Next, it's time to find what lights you up! Passion is really the fuel that keeps the Blue Flame lit. Passion can feel like a bit of a loaded word, one that gets tossed around so much, it's easy to write off as just some self-help babble. But think of it as *activities that you find invigorating.* Luckily for us, it's kind of easy to identify. Let's start by looking at activities that seem to absorb you completely. Can you think of anything that you love doing so much you lose track of time?

Joshua: Does binge-watching *The Office* count?

Alicia: Haha, no, but I have a little exercise to help us. Are you willing to follow my lead, and trust me?

Joshua: Yes

Alicia: Okay, close your eyes.

Alicia paused to let Joshua sit in silence for a moment. Leaders like Alicia must be comfortable leaning into the discomfort of exercises like guided visualizations. These might feel unusual in the workplace—even silly—but the brain science and practice show that visualization exercises like this can be truly transformative.

Alicia: Let's take a walk down memory lane. Think back to your earliest memory, usually around age three or four. What was it?

Joshua's eyes remained closed.

Joshua: Probably the excitement of learning to ride my bike. It was exhilarating once I got it.

Alicia: Good. Now slowly start moving toward the present. It's almost like you're replaying the movie of your life in your head. Think about your life's journey: the ups and downs, the tragedies and triumphs, and feel free to close your eyes for a few minutes as you do so. As you are recalling your life story, put a pin on moments that really stand out along the way. Ones where you felt the most alive. Ones where you were completely invigorated by what you were doing. What were you doing? Who was with you? What did it feel like?

Joshua settled into the exercise, clearly taking it seriously. Alicia stayed quiet for several minutes so that Joshua could take his time. Sensing that Joshua was back somewhere close to the present day, she interjected.

Alicia: Okay, now slowly come back and open your eyes.

As Joshua came to, Alicia could see his eyes were clearer than they were before.

Joshua: Wow. That was powerful. It's not everyday that we stop to replay our own story. One early memory that jumped out to me was my first skiing holiday. My parents are big skiers. My brother Zak was too. And when I got the hang of it, it was heaven. Just being able to move through space like that, at that speed. I felt like I could fly! I was completely swept away by the feeling—my parents had to drag me off the slopes at the end of the day! I think it was the physicality and the challenge of it that was so invigorating.

Alicia smiled because she knew they were getting somewhere, but weren't quite there yet. She took a mental note of the characteristics that made this particular experience feel invigorating—physicality, an element of challenge—*but continued on the hunt for themes. Themes expose themselves when you can observe the characteristics that several peak moments (of the type that Joshua described in the skiing example) share in common.*

Alicia: Born to ski it seems! What other times in your life gave you this same feeling of freedom, excitement, and exhilaration?

Joshua: That would be writing. I distinctly remember a time when a teacher gave us a creative writing exercise in middle school. I must have been eleven years old. I wrote something crazy about pirates. But I remember I was totally absorbed. I kept writing, even after my mom tucked me in, and I fell asleep with my pen in my hand. I woke up and began writing immediately. That still happens when I'm working on my novel.

Alicia: What is it about writing that has this effect on you?

Joshua: It allows me to be so imaginative, it lights me ...

He paused and smirked because he realized what he was about to say.

Joshua: It really does light me up. I get to use my imagination, my love of language, and the challenge of synthesizing my thoughts into words—if I'm successful, I will connect with my readers in a meaningful way. I guess you could say that because of my talents, I have developed somewhat of a passion for writing.

Alicia: That's well put! Writing is definitely something that evokes passion for you, and you're right to point out that your talents and passions can be mutually reinforcing. But let's keep looking: what other specific events stand out to you because you felt full of life and excitement?

Joshua: Well, I think winning the championship with the skiing team has to be up there. It just felt like a public acknowledgment of the fact that I was good at this and that I'd put in so much effort. And then knowing that I'd delivered for the team and that I hadn't let them down felt great. More recently, I feel pretty good about my personal best in the marathon. I run for fun, pretty much every day, but I also run the Denver marathon and half marathon and raise money for a charity—a shelter for the homeless. I'm not that fast but I completed it in under four hours. That felt good, and I remember that feeling! And then going back a bit further, graduation. I really wanted a good degree and worked hard at it, and when I graduated with a 3.8 that felt like a big win.

Alicia: Do you see a theme here? What do the moments when you feel completely invigorated seem to share in common?

Joshua: I think it's the challenge. I have a clear goal in mind and I'm doing something I love, but I'm really pushing myself. When I'm pushing myself in pursuit of a worthy goal, nothing else seems to matter. I get very committed and focused. But what is becoming much clearer to me is that I get totally into the zone when I'm taking in information and ideas, and spitting back out a really tightly packaged rearticulation of those ideas. I guess it is this synthesis thing we talked about earlier. But something I'm realizing now is that one of the reasons why I find that invigorating is because it helps me to connect directly with my audience, and connect them with new ideas in a way that is easy for them to understand.

Alicia began to make notes on the whiteboard to capture the key themes that were emerging when it came to things that tended to light Joshua up. She wrote down "pushing myself in pursuit of a worthy goal," "synthesizing ideas, and translating those ideas into words that connect." She couldn't help but notice the connection between Joshua's talents and passions, which made sense given that talents and passion tend to be mutually reinforcing.

3. FIND THEIR PURPOSE
Now that we understand what someone's talents and passions are, it's important to uncover what they care deeply about, what brings them a sense of meaning. We call this "purpose." If talents are the kindling of the Blue Flame and passions are the fuel, then Purpose is the spark that ignites it. It tends to be the case that the things we care deeply about stem from an innate desire to help others. There's some interesting research about how we humans are wired for altruism and derive intrinsic motivation from helping others (see Chapter 9). So it's important to have them look outward and explore the things externally—people, causes, suffering—they feel the deepest emotional connection to.

> **Alicia:** It's time to get even more personal. I want to find out what has real meaning for you, and what you care deeply about. Given that we humans have a deep biological longing to help others, to find what we really care deeply about, one place to go look is toward the suffering, injustice, or hardship that other people experience. This may feel odd, but if I asked you what kind of suffering you would most desire to alleviate—in your community, in the world—what would it be?
>
> **Joshua:** I guess the first thing that comes to mind is my older brother, Zak. He went off the rails in college. I mean seriously off the rails. And he suffered a lot. He got into drugs and stuff and then he dropped out of college. And he felt he couldn't face our mom and dad because he'd let them down. But he still had a phone at that time and he finally agreed to meet me for a coffee. We sat on a bench in the park. I remember him wolfing down the muffins I'd brought. He looked awful. And that was the last time I saw him. After that, he went completely off the radar.

Joshua stared into space for a while and Alicia said nothing, holding the moment. Alicia recognized that silence of this sort is okay, and that her job was to hold the space for Joshua to process this at his own pace.

Joshua: A friend told me he saw him sleeping on the street, you know, in a shop doorway or something. This was a couple of years ago. Since then we've heard nothing. So he could still be sleeping on the streets in Denver, or maybe he's left town, or maybe he's dead. I have no idea. So, in terms of suffering in our society, I hope to address homelessness. And I do, in a small way, by running for charities that support the homeless population. I drop in and volunteer at their shelter every now and again, too. I hope one day, in this work, he will show back up and we can reunite.

Alicia: I'm so sorry. Thank you for sharing that. These Blue Flame conversations often get very emotional because we're talking about our truth, so thank you again for sharing yours. Do you mind if we continue or do you need a moment?

Joshua: I'm good, thanks for listening. Let's keep moving.

Alicia: You might be wondering how this thread you just shared about your brother relates. The Blue Flame is a process, and it is important that we move through it in this order—talents, passions, purpose, impact. If we rewind to the passions we spoke about earlier, I wrote down skiing, running, writing, and communicating as experiences that you found invigorating. Now, what's most important is that we look within these experiences to understand why you're so passionate about them. If you could explain the distilled reason these activities seem to light you up, what would you say?

Joshua: I feel like writing—or communicating—lights me up because I can use my imagination to come up with the best way to convey a message to another person. And for skiing and running, I guess I love picking bold goals and then working toward them intently.

Alicia: So, in the same way that we just drilled into your favorite activities to find what, at a deeper level, makes these activities feel so invigorating, it is important to dig a bit deeper into this sense of meaning you find in addressing homelessness.

Joshua: Hmm. I guess that every time someone new walks into the shelter for help, I feel like I'm looking at someone who has become invisible, and I feel like I'm looking at my lost brother. It creates within me this overwhelming desire to make people see them again. I want to help them tell their stories so that people can connect with them and see them as real people. This is how I'd like to use my passion for synthesis and connecting with people through words.

Throughout the conversation, Alicia had been paying close attention to not only the words Joshua said, but also the information conveyed by his intonation, body language, and other non-verbal cues. This is a skill that leaders can work to develop. It allows us to pick up on a lot of signals from these non-verbal cues that words themselves often don't capture. In this case, noticing that Joshua's voice quivered a bit and his tone of voice softened and felt almost tender signaled to Alicia that this cause struck a real emotional chord with him. Not only did she notice it visually, but she could feel it.

Alicia: I understand. So what is really behind this feeling is the urge to help give a voice to people who you feel have been silenced, to help the unseen be seen. I noticed in your body language how much that resonated with you as you just described it.

Joshua: Wow, yes, that's it.

Alicia: Yes, that seems to be a very important part of your Blue Flame. It's clearly something that you care deeply about. Something that has a deeper meaning for you.

In a live Blue Flame conversation, you would want to stay on the topic of Purpose longer. What else might be there? Use the questions on page 158, like "What else do you feel most connected to?" This could help to reveal other things that give Joshua a deeper sense of purpose.

Alicia: Now comes the fun part. You'll remember that the Blue Flame sits at the intersection point of your talents, your passions, and your purpose. Let's look back at what came out of each of those segments of our discussion, and start to see if anything comes into clearer view for you. We discussed your talents—synthesis, communication, empathy, and discipline. In our discussions on passions, you talked about writing, connecting with others, and running, as well as setting lofty goals and working toward them. And you really lit up when we started talking about the sense of meaning you find in the idea of giving people a voice.

Discovering your Blue Flame is useless if you're not going to use it to elevate your impact. Now that Joshua had a clearer understanding of his talents, his passions, and his purpose, Alicia and Joshua could start to discuss the ways in which Joshua's Blue Flame can be applied to the greatest effect, within the company and beyond.

But Blue Flame leaders should be careful not to rush these conversations. In this particular instance, Alicia decided it was best—given the emotional nature of some of their conversations and the epiphanies Joshua was having—to end the meeting for the day and reconvene a couple of days later once all the information had settled in.

4. FIND THEIR AREA OF GREATEST IMPACT
Joshua and Alicia reconvened a few days later.

> **Alicia:** I want to start today by telling a story. Three years ago I was walking back from getting groceries. I was crossing the street when a guy blew through the stop sign going fifty. He was so close to me that he clipped my grocery bag and sent a small watermelon flying through the air. I watched it splatter onto the asphalt. Amid the shock of the moment, I had what can only be described as an amazing epiphany, one that ended up being an incredible gift: the realization that my time could be up at any moment. I had always known this, somewhere in my head, but this moment really made me feel it and integrate this understanding into my body and my mind in a way I hadn't ever before. It hit much closer to home—literally, I'm afraid.
>
> Unfortunately, this is common. Many of us don't appreciate life until death or something like it strikes painfully close to home. My experience taught me that recognizing how precious life is can give us an energy, a vibrancy, and a motivation to *live*. It can spark in us a real urge to make the most of the time that we do have. And looking at your life and your career through this lens can be game-changing.
>
> As we mentioned in Chapter 10, there are a few amazing quotes that do a wonderful job of helping us to understand and internalize the power of reflecting on our own mortality in this way:
>
> > "Many people die with their music still in them. Why is this so? Too often it is because they are always getting ready to live. Before they know it, time runs out." — Oliver Wendell Holmes

"Remembering that I'll be dead soon is the most important tool I've ever encountered to help me make the big choices in life. Because almost everything—all external expectations, all pride, all fear of embarrassment or failure—these things just fall away in the face of death, leaving only what is truly important." — *Steve Jobs*

Joshua: Yeah, I've always liked the quote by Mary Oliver, "What is it you plan to do with your one wild and precious life?" That word "precious" always struck a chord with me.

Alicia: Exactly. So, today, I'd like you to explore that same idea. Forget about your current job for the moment. Now that you have gotten clearer on your Blue Flame, think about what you *really* want to spend your life doing with it. What you want to make of your "one wild and precious life"?

To do this, it helps to begin with the end in mind. Imagine you're at your own retirement party. I don't know what you'll be retiring *from*; it could be this company, or it could be something entirely different. Imagine that everyone is coming up to say a few words. What do you want them to say about how you showed up? How you made them feel? What do you want them to say about your impact on them, the company, or the world? Take some time to think about it.

Joshua was silent for a few minutes.

Joshua: You know, a big realization I'm having is that my talents lend themselves to being a damn good writer, and some of my highest of highs have been when I've been lost in my writing. So it's definitely what I do best and it's certainly what lights me up. I also care deeply about connecting with other people—it brings me a sense of meaning—and writing is a way to do that. But the thing is, I don't think I'm using that in a way that is having a great impact today. I'm definitely not using it to give people a voice.

Alicia: Yes, that's common. We naturally tend to gravitate toward things we are good at, like writing, but we often fail to realize it's important to look around at how to best use those talents so we can have the largest and most positive impacts on the areas that are important to us.

Joshua was clearly having a realization of some kind.

Joshua: At my retirement party, I want people to be able to say that Joshua helped give people a voice—especially those who haven't been fully heard—so that they could realize their full potential. I want to be remembered as a guy who put his talent and passion for writing to good use by helping underrepresented people find better lives. If I can look back and feel I've done that, I will feel I've achieved something. You know—even if I won't be able to help my brother, I will still have helped a lot of other people.

Alicia: I can see now you're gaining some clarity on how all these aspects of yourself can work together. Let's zoom back out now. We have covered a lot of ground in this conversation. I'm going to give you my perspective and see if it can inspire some new thoughts. As you know, what originally brought us to this conversation was the fact that you're not really on fire here at work. You're not fulfilling your potential. Given what you've just told me about your goals and your retirement party, that's a bit surprising! All the ingredients should be there for you to be totally fired up. Am I right?

Joshua: I enjoy some of the work. I really do. I enjoy crafting good marketing materials, and writing PR releases, and helping the team to work with our outside agencies on the next marketing campaign. I love working on our videos and podcasts and so on. It's really challenging and creative. It's just ... Some of the things we have to do—I know they have to get done, but I can't get excited about them. Updating the sales materials with the latest technical advances, analyzing our web traffic and our email campaigns, I know it's what I signed up for when I started a career in marketing, but ...

I wanted to work here so that I could make a difference, and I can't always see the difference I'm making. I help create marketing campaigns, and maybe a year later we land a new account and I think, "Did I help do that?" I help craft sales materials, and technical materials for the accounts team, and I hear about new business coming in or clients giving us new projects, but I don't get a direct buzz out of that. I don't feel plugged into the actual changemaking events. Does that make sense? I feel that I'm part of the effort, which is a good feeling, but I'm not getting the same rush. I'm not crossing the finishing line and looking at my time on the clock and lifting my arms and shouting, "Yes!" And right now, I don't think people at the retirement party would be saying that I made a significant contribution to developing a new drug or a strain of rice that feeds starving people.

Right then, Alicia had a realization. As is oftentimes the case when people aren't lit up by the work they are doing, Joshua couldn't see clearly the connection between the work he is doing, and the way that it is making other people's—in this case, customers'—lives better. Alicia recognized that it is her job, as a leader, to help create that connection and keep it visible for Joshua.

> **Alicia:** Thank you for your honesty. The good news is you have the potential to make a significant contribution here. If we don't have successful marketing, we don't have a company and we can't help people develop those new drugs and food and clean energy. What we really need is to get you plugged into the impact that the work you are doing is having on our customers. When you can see the impact that your work is having on others, I'm guessing we can start to see all that wonderful energy of yours again, and have it lighting up our whole company.
>
> **Joshua:** That sounds amazing. How do we make that happen?

Now is when your organizational knowledge and talent-agent skills need to come into the picture. Alicia began scanning through her vast knowledge of the needs of the organization to help identify those needs that aligned with Joshua's Blue Flame.

Now it is conceivable that, at this point in the conversation, it becomes clear that the person's Blue Flame and the needs of the organization are not a great fit. That's okay! It wouldn't mean Joshua is a bad employee, or the company a bad employer. But when we find ourselves in this place—and you inevitably will as a leader—you should start thinking about companies or organizations that could allow your teammate's Blue Flame to burn much brighter. Ask yourself, "How can I help my teammate to find the place where their Blue Flame can have the greatest impact on the world—even if that is outside of our organization?"

However, assuming there are ways that your teammate's Blue Flame can be applied in your business with big impact, you may find yourself needing to think about how you might recraft their role in order to bring it closer to the intersection point of their talents, passions, and purpose—or redeploy them into a new role altogether. Doing so requires that you drill down into the parts of the current role that aren't aligned with their greatest talents and passions—and consider how you might remove some of those from their plate, while stacking it full of new activities that are a closer fit with their Blue Flame. This is called job recrafting.

Here's what I mean:

Alicia: Okay, so you love writing things: collateral, sales copy, videos, articles, and so on. You love creating, crafting, and communicating.

Joshua: Yes! It lights me up almost every time.

Alicia: Okay, and analyzing the return on ad spend for a trade press campaign?

Joshua: Not so much. But, you know, you can't write a book without doing the proofread and the spell-check. There's always stuff that has to be done.

Alicia: You're right. And it is certainly possible to get deeply involved in tasks that are tedious and unrewarding on the face of it, if you remind yourself what the purpose is. I think we can help you feel that way about pretty much every aspect of your job. But I'm going to make a few suggestions that I think can help bring us closer to the goal of helping you find your fire again.

What is your position?

Joshua: I am the marketing manager.

Alicia: That means that you are accountable for delivering on our marketing objectives. And if you do that, I'm happy. But I don't mind exactly *how* you do that. You, as the leader, need to lead the team to deliver the objectives and grow the team along the way. But exactly how you divide up the workload or go about it is entirely up to you.

Rather than solving this for Joshua—a well-intentioned but disempowering leadership tendency—Alicia was empowering Joshua to figure out how to move closer to his Blue Flame himself. But, at this point in the conversation, you can offer collaboration. As the leader, start to elicit your teammates' best thinking on how they can move closer to their Blue Flame, and offer your own.

Alicia: So let me offer some thoughts as to how to draw on the principles of the Blue Flame to do that.

Joshua: Okay, great. I'd love some tips.

Alicia: My first suggestion is to refocus on the things that light you up—the writing, the videos, the podcasts, the campaigns. Throw yourself into those and find ways to delegate anything else to your team members. Maybe this won't be the tactic forever, but we need you to get your mojo back. Let's get the things that drain you off your plate—just make sure they get done. How does that sound?

Joshua: Uh—that sounds like heaven. That's my dream job. It also makes me feel guilty.

Alicia: Why?

Joshua: Because I'll be having nothing but fun and I will feel as if I'm asking the team to pick up everything else.

Alicia: Well, you're the manager, so you still have to be *across* all the other activities that need to get done to hit our goals. You have to make sure they are happening, and happening with the degree of excellence that we need to hit our targets. And you have to do your bit, sure—but here's the other thing. My second suggestion is to improve your delegation and decrease your guilt by having Blue Flame conversations with everyone on your team.

Joshua: Whoa.

Alicia: Yeah. Pay it forward, if you will. Join me in the quest to light this whole organization ablaze with Blue Flames! In fact, come to think of it, this should be an expectation of *all* managers in our organization. After all, our business is just a collection of people, and in order to make the mark on the world that we are trying to make, we need all of our people to be lit up!

In the same way that we have done, explore their talents, their passions, and their purpose, then help them discover where they can have the biggest impact. Try to organize your team in a way that brings each person as close to their Blue Flame as possible. I know it's a relatively small team, but I'll bet my bottom dollar that you will have someone on the team—just by way of example—who absolutely loves analyzing return on ad spend for a trade press campaign. Loves it! Get them to focus on that. Get everyone focusing on the types of things that they can do best, that invigorate them, and that they care deeply about.

I'm even happy to get you a copy of *The Blue Flame*, and sponsor you to go take the training that teaches leaders how to have Blue Flame conversations and get the best out of their people. Do you think you can do that?

Joshua: I can do that!

Things began to click into place for Joshua. Helping his team find their Blue Flame could be the ticket to helping him lean into his Blue Flame, he realized. It could also be the ticket to helping his team to come alive and start delivering the types of results he knew were possible—and that Alicia really wanted to see.

Alicia: Thirdly—now this is really important—I'm going to help you get plugged into the client- and market-facing parts of our company to see the impact of the work we do firsthand. I'd like you to spend more time with the account management team, with the sales team, with the tech team, *and* with our clients. I'll explain this to the heads of each department and then I want you to reach out to people and start spending time with them. I think that this will help you turn what we do into wonderful stories that will bring the company to life for all our stakeholders. The problem is not that you're not having an impact, it's that you haven't been able to see the impact. I'll take the blame for that but I'm ready to fix it.

Even though this conversation was for your benefit, it's clear that I have had a realization about how I can do better. I can now see that in order for you to tell the best stories—and in order for you to feel really lit up by the work that you're doing—you need to know exactly how our work improves people's lives.

Alicia realized that Joshua was suffering from a challenge that, unfortunately, is all too common in the working world: our people can't see the connection between the work they are doing and the impact on the people and communities that their work is serving. Remember, every business exists to serve someone, and when we can draw the connection brightly and vividly for our people, it can imbue their work with greater meaning and elicit greater discretionary effort.

Alicia: Next, there is a concrete step we can take to help address your sense of purpose of giving people a voice. First, I think we should enlist our CEO to help. I'll talk to Rachael and set up a meeting. I want you to talk to her about the homeless in Denver, maybe about your brother, and see if she'd be interested in getting the company involved. Our company has made a commitment to being good corporate citizens here in Denver, and as a lifeline resident of Denver, I'm guessing this will strike a chord with her. With the blessing of the CEO, you can start enlisting other colleagues to volunteer or help fundraise. I'm not promising anything, but I have a feeling she'll give you a favorable response.

Don't limit yourself or your company to thinking that endeavors like this don't improve your bottom line. They can sometimes in very direct ways, but they also foster a rich culture of fulfilled people on fire who have a connection to your company and want to do great work for you. If you empower people to do what brings them deeper meaning, they will give you a lot more discretionary effort.

Joshua: That's a great idea, I hope she'll be into it.

Alicia: Secondly, we should also talk to her about a new intern program. Maybe some people at the homeless shelter or their kids could use help getting back into work and into the community. With paid internships and new opportunities, you could really make a difference and give voice, and opportunity, to people who feel voiceless.

Joshua was beaming from ear to ear. You might be thinking, "Yeah, but we can't do this sort of thing for every employee." My answer is, "Why not?"

Having had dozens of Blue Flame conversations, I will assure you that investing time in these talks can make for some of the highest return-on-time meetings you will have as a leader.

After all, remember that a business is nothing more than people working with other people to do stuff for other people. If you want your business to be successful, you need people who are on fire, right?

Alicia handed the whiteboard marker to Joshua. It was his chance to write his own Blue Flame Statement. Drawing on all of the other notes that still remained on the board from the earlier segments of the conversation, and referring to his handy Blue Flame Statement worksheet from MyBlueFlame.com, Joshua did what he does best—he put his heart into words:

With imagination, energy and the powerful use of language, Joshua helps give voice to and create connection with the stories of the voiceless, so that everyone can have an opportunity to be heard, be seen, and feel connected.

★ ★ ★

Joshua left the meeting room, his Blue Flame already burning considerably brighter than the faint glimmer from before. Alicia did not see an overnight transformation—and you may not either—but helping someone like Joshua to discover and lay a path to follow their Blue Flame is *the* first step. It is the spark. Your job as a leader then becomes to keep it lit, and help stoke the flames as time goes on.

Inspired by his newfound sense of clarity and energy, Joshua started spending time with each department and began to understand more clearly the impact that their work was having on customers' lives.

He reached out to people and communities that had been directly affected by the company's products, and began to craft stories that showed how even the most technical aspects of the company's work turned into innovative products that improved people's lives: new drugs, new food, and new biofuels.

Joshua's new storytelling angle helped breathe greater meaning into not only his immediate team, but the whole company. Joshua posted his stories on the company's intranet and salespeople, account managers, programmers, and biologists read them with pride. The whole company became reenergized as they saw more clearly the positive impact that the work they were doing was having on real people. As is often the case, many people in the company had lost sight of this.

Joshua and his team began to incorporate these stories into their marketing, and trained the sales team on selling using the power of storytelling. It turns out that the stories resonated strongly with clients.

As some of these proof points started to accumulate, it became clear to Joshua how he could use his talents, passions, and purpose to have a far greater impact within the company.

But this impact didn't end with Joshua. As he rediscovered his own energy, it had an immediate, positive ripple effect on his team. When leaders find their own Blue Flames, it sets a new "tone at the top." He went on to learn how to conduct Blue Flame conversations himself, and as he helped his team to discover and lean into their own Blue Flames, he began to get more out of them, while helping them to love their work more. Joshua felt that he and his team were the beautiful shiny "after" shots on one of those weight loss commercials.

As for Alicia, her marketing team went from being a time-suck to a performance engine. Her team's performance—and by extension, *her* performance as a leader—improved. Everyone's stress went down, and everyone enjoyed their work more.

But it wasn't just about performance for Alicia. She aspired to be the type of leader who was known for getting the best out of her people. This mattered to her as she thought about the ding she was trying to put in the universe. At her retirement party, she was hopeful people would comment on how she got the best out of her team. The Blue Flame conversation, it turns out, was a simple but powerful tool she could use to lean into *her own* area of greatest impact.

While these Blue Flame conversations aren't a cure-all—after all, effective leadership is multifaceted—they are a crucial step in the direction of building a high-performing, engaged team. As Alicia realized, and as I have seen so clearly firsthand in my own leadership, life can be so much better and results so much more attainable when our teammates are playing in the zones that align with their talents, passions, and purpose.

She also realized that other leaders in the company will start to take note. "There's something interesting going on over there in marketing!" they whispered. Pretty soon, other leaders were knocking on her door asking, "What kind of Wheaties have you been feeding the marketing team?" Her team became an inspiring case study of what happens when leaders embrace the Blue Flame, and make a commitment to bringing the idea to life in their own organization.

When other leaders catch on to the impact it can have, and lean into the same commitment, the impact can spread like wildfire within a business—and beyond.

Acknowledgments

Writing this book was harder than a rock on a cold day. Tougher than I ever imagined. But the deeper I got into the research and writing, the more I realized just how worthy of a cause this is—and how rewarding it is to have the chance to package and share ideas that can help other leaders to expand their impact.

I believe, deep in my bones, that the Blue Flame has the power to change the trajectory of lives and transform the way we think about leadership. And even if this thing impacts only a few leaders, and they go on to impact just a few of their teammates... then the late nights of writing, early mornings of research, and newly sprouted gray hairs will have all been well worth it.

Even though my editor insisted that it is my name that needs to go on the cover of the book, there's a whole tribe of people who are as deserving of that real estate.

I have to start by thanking my awesome wife, Courtney. You have been supportive at every step. Thanks for giving me the space to hunker down in my office for evenings on end (and graciously covering dinner duty!) so that I could bring this message to the world. I draw a ton of inspiration from seeing you leaning into your own Blue Flame in your career. Thank you so much for your support, encouragement, and patience.

To my family, who has always supported my pursuit of things that I found energizing and fulfilling, even when those things were a bit—ahem—weird. (Cue the tape of my infamous homemade puppet shows.)

A hearty "thank you" to everyone on my publishing team. At times during this process, I felt like I was lost in the cold, dark woods of first-time authoring... but then I quickly remembered I had a whole team by my side. And there you were with a flashlight. Your support and guidance always seemed to arrive at just the right time. To Jonathan Gifford, for your witty writing, patience, and relentless positivity. To Josh Raab, for smoothing my writing with your proverbial rolling pin, and helping me get this book to the finish line step-by-step. To Amélie Cherlin, for making sure the manuscript was in tip-top shape and helping me realize how much I love the em dash. To Andrew Bell, for his thoughtful book design. To Jordan Walczak, who helped bring the concepts to life with the sketch pencil. And to the others who worked behind the scenes to make this book possible.

The Blue Flame wouldn't have happened without the years of partnership and support from the awesome crew at Alpine Investors. Working with you has been one of the great blessings in my life, has given me much of the raw material that formed the foundation for this book, and has helped me to discover and lean into my own Blue Flame. I'm so proud and grateful to have had the opportunity to work with and learn from such an amazing and talented group of leaders.

And finally, thanks to the countless leaders who I have had the chance to learn from along my own professional journey—those I have had the opportunity to lead and be led by, and those whose leadership I've watched from a distance. I'm especially thankful for those of you who are as committed as I am to making the workplace a force for good in the lives of our employees. The world needs more leaders like you who are committed to helping their people be their best.

www.ingramcontent.com/pod-product-compliance
Lightning Source LLC
Chambersburg PA
CBHW071357210526
45465CB00001B/142